Workbook

Diesel
Technology
Fundamentals, Service, Repair

Eighth Edition

by
Andrew Norman

Publisher
The Goodheart-Willcox Company, Inc.
Tinley Park, IL
www.g-w.com

Table of Contents

Introduction

The *Workbook for Diesel Technology* provides a thorough guide to accompany the *Diesel Technology* textbook. It highlights information, improves understanding, and simplifies the contents of the text. Answering the workbook questions will help you remember important ideas and concepts covered in the *Diesel Technology* textbook.

The workbook contains questions that serve as an additional study guide to *Diesel Technology*. The workbook units correlate with those in the textbook. The order of the questions follows the sequence of the textbook material. This will make it easier for you to find information in the text and also to check your answers.

It is recommended that before you attempt to answer questions in this workbook, you should study the *Diesel Technology* textbook first. After studying the textbook, try to answer as many of the workbook questions as possible without referring to the text. Answer any remaining questions by referring to the appropriate areas in the textbook chapter.

By studying the *Diesel Technology* textbook and finishing the workbook, you will develop a solid background in diesel engines. Additional knowledge and experience can be gained by hands-on experience. You should take every opportunity to learn all you can about diesel engines.

Andrew Norman

Instructions for Answering Workbook Questions

Each chapter in this workbook directly correlates to the same chapter in the text. Before answering the questions in the workbook, study the assigned chapter in the text and answer the end-of-chapter review questions. Then, review the objectives at the beginning of each workbook chapter. This will help you review the important concepts presented in the chapter. Try to complete as many workbook questions as possible without referring to the textbook. Then, use the text to complete the remaining questions.

A variety of questions are used in the workbook including multiple choice, identification, completion, and short answer. These questions should be answered in the following manner:

Multiple Choice

Select the best answer and write the correct answer in the blank.

1. One-piece cylinder block construction is used on what major classification of diesel engine?

    (A) Mobile.

    (B) Two-cycle.

    (C) Large stationary.

    (D) Four-cycle.

1. <u>(A) Mobile</u>

Completion

In the blank provided, write the word or words that best complete the statement.

2. The continuous flow of fuel through the injector prevents _____ _____ from forming in the fuel system.

2. <u>air pockets</u>

Identification

Identify the components indicated on the illustration or photograph accompanying the question.

3. Identify the parts of the diesel engine cylinder wet liner illustrated below.
    (A) _Cylinder liner_
    (B) _Seal ring grooves_
    (C) _Seal rings_
    (D) _Crevice seal_
    (E) _Crevice seal groove_

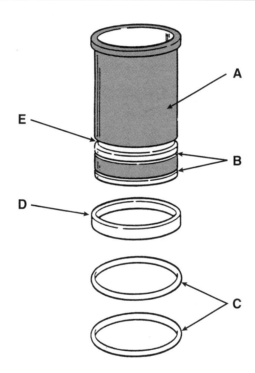

Short Answer

Provide complete responses to the statements.

4. Why is it important to keep hand tools free of oil and grease?
    To prevent slippage that can cause injury; to have a professional appearance.

Matching

Match the term in the left column with its description. Place the corresponding letter and answer in the blank.

Match the following pumps with their correct definitions.

    (A) Individual jerk pump

    (B) Multiple-plunger inline pump

    (C) Unit injector

    (D) Pressure-time injection

    (E) Distributor pump injection

5. Contained in its own housing and serving a single cylinder.

    5. _(A) Individual jerk pump_

6. Uses a spinning rotor to distribute pressurized fuel to the individual injectors in the proper cylinder firing sequence.

    6. _(E) Distributor pump injection_

7. Uses a number of individual jerk pumps contained in one common housing.

    7. _(B) Multiple-plunger inline pump_

8. Fuel metering is controlled by engine speed and fuel pressure.

    8. _(D) Pressure-time injection_

9. Times, atomizes, meters, and pressurizes the fuel within the injector body or unit serving each cylinder.

    9. _(C) Unit injector_

Other Types of Questions

When other types of workbook questions are presented, follow the specific instructions that accompany the problem.

Name _____

Date _____

Instructor _____

Score _____ Text pages 15–26

Chapter 1

Introduction to Diesel Engines

After studying this chapter and completing supplemental exercises, you will be able to:

- List five reasons diesel engines are more efficient than gasoline engines.
- Define and explain how compression ignition is used in a diesel engine.
- Name two major advantages and disadvantages of diesel fuel.
- Explain in simple terms how electronic engine controls work and why they have been introduced on all modern mobile diesel engines.
- Name the major applications for diesel engines in modern industry and transportation.
- Name several key milestones in the development of the diesel engine.

Diesel versus Gasoline Engines

1. The gasoline engine and diesel engine are two examples of _____ combustion engines.

1. _____

2. A diesel engine uses the _____ _____ _____ to ignite the fuel charge in the combustion chamber.

2. _____

3. List some of the basic ways gasoline and diesel engines are similar to one another.

_____

_____

_____

4. Technician A states that diesel and gasoline engines
can be designed to operate on a four-stroke or two-stroke
cycle. Technician B states that gasoline engines are only
designed as four-stroke engines. Who is correct?

4. _____

   (A) A only.
   (B) B only.
   (C) Both A & B.
   (D) Neither A nor B.

5. Name the four piston strokes of a four-stroke cycle engine.

   _____

   _____

   _____

   _____

6. Technician A says that virtually all high-horsepower
gasoline engines are four-cycle engines. Technician B
states that both four-cycle and two-cycle diesel engines
have been used successfully in high-horsepower
applications. Who is correct?

6. _____

   (A) A only.
   (B) B only.
   (C) Both A & B.
   (D) Neither A nor B.

7. In a two-cycle diesel engine, intake and compression
occur on the _____ piston stroke, while power and
exhaust occur during the downward stroke.

7. _____

8. List four reasons diesel engines are more efficient than gasoline engines.

   _____

   _____

   _____

   _____

9. Technician A states that in a diesel engine, the liquid
diesel fuel is not premixed with air prior to entering
the combustion chamber. Technician B states that air is
taken into the diesel engine cylinder through the intake
manifold and compressed, which heats the air prior to
the injection of diesel fuel. Who is correct?

9. _____

   (A) A only.
   (B) B only.
   (C) Both A & B.
   (D) Neither A nor B.

Name _____

10. Technician A says in a carbureted or fuel-injected   10. _____
    gasoline engine, speed is controlled by regulating the
    amount of intake air mixed with fuel that is delivered
    to the cylinders. Technician B states that both gasoline
    and diesel engines use a throttling valve in the engine's
    intake manifold. Who is correct?
    (A) A only.
    (B) B only.
    (C) Both A & B.
    (D) Neither A nor B.

11. _____ _____ in a diesel engine intake manifold remains   11. _____
    constant at all loads.

12. In a diesel engine, engine speed is controlled by   12. _____
    varying the amount of _____ injected into each
    cylinder.

13. List three of the common ways of controlling the amount of diesel fuel injected into an
    engine cylinder.

    _____

    _____

14. All on-highway diesel engine manufacturers currently   14. _____
    incorporate the _____ _____ function into the
    engine's electronic control system instead of using a
    mechanically operated governor.
    (A) lubrication system
    (B) fuel governing
    (C) air suspension
    (D) None of the above.

15. A governor is a device capable of sensing engine   15. _____
    _____ and _____ and changing fuel delivery amounts
    accordingly.

16. Before the advent of electronic-controlled diesel fuel injection systems, what were three ways
    that a diesel engine governor was controlled?

    _____

    _____

    _____

17. An engine's _____ _____ compares the volume of air   17. _____
    in a cylinder before compression with its volume after
    compression.

18. Diesel engines operate at _____ (higher, lower)   18. _____
    compression ratios than gasoline engines.

19. Technician A states that typical diesel compression
ratios range from 16:1 to 24:1. Technician B states
that diesel engine compression ratios are more in the
range of 7.5:1 to 9.5:1. Who is correct?

    (A) A only.

    (B) B only.

    (C) Both A & B.

    (D) Neither A nor B.

19. _____

20. Diesel fuel contains _____ (more, less) heat energy
(BTU) than gasoline.

20. _____

21. While a gasoline engine converts only about 25% of its
fuel energy into usable power, fuel efficiency in diesel
engines can be as high as _____%.

21. _____

22. A typical heavy-duty truck diesel engine can run for
_____ miles before it must be rebuilt, and the same
engine can be successfully rebuilt many times.

22. _____

23. List three of the drawbacks of diesel engines when compared to gasoline engines.

_____

_____

_____

24. How do extremes in temperature adversely affect diesel fuel?

_____

_____

_____

_____

_____

Diesel Engine History

25. _____ _____ is credited with the invention of the diesel
engine.

25. _____

26. _____ _____ is credited with the invention of the
modern gasoline engine.

26. _____

27. The inventor of the diesel engine first proposed in
his 1892 patent draft that_____ _____ be the engine's
probable fuel.

27. _____

28. In the earliest diesel engines, an air-blast system using
a(n) _____ _____ from a refrigerator was used to
vaporize the fuel.

28. _____

Name _____

29. During the 1920s, a major milestone was passed when the Robert Bosch company developed a compact, reliable _____ _____ _____ for diesel engines.

29. _____

30. During the 1950s, the development of the compact Roosa Master _____ _____ paved the way for diesel-powered farm tractors and agricultural equipment.

30. _____

31. Name the two broad categories of modern diesel engine applications.

_____

_____

32. Diesel engines can drive external accessories, such as a tractor engine powering a hay baler, through the use of a(n) _____ _____.

32. _____

33. In _____ applications, a powertrain is used to convert engine speed into the machine speed.

33. _____

34. List six common mobile applications for modern diesel engines.

_____

_____

_____

_____

_____

_____

35. List four common stationary applications for modern diesel engines.

_____

_____

_____

_____

36. Concerns of diesel exhaust emissions led to the development of _____.
    (A) electronic engine controls
    (B) exhaust emission equipment
    (C) more stringent air pollution laws
    (D) All of the above.

36. _____

37. To increase engine output and responsiveness, many modern diesel engines are equipped with turbochargers or _____.

37. _____

38. The use of _____ _____ _____ in modern diesel
    engines results in a 3%–5% fuel improvement
    and decreased emissions.

38. _____

39. Improvements to _____ fuel injectors and _____
    _____ injection systems have led to system designs
    capable of attaining higher injection pressures than
    earlier diesel fuel injection systems.

39. _____

40. List three recent diesel engine design advances that have increased diesel engine performance.

    _____

    _____

    _____

Name _____

Date _____

Instructor _____

Score _____ Text pages 27–36

Chapter 2
Shop Safety

After studying this chapter and completing supplemental exercises, you will be able to:

- Explain the importance of shop safety in a repair shop.
- Describe the personal safety precautions that a technician must follow.
- Outline the general shop housekeeping procedures that must be maintained.
- Explain the safety rules that must be practiced when working with fuel injectors.
- Describe the three basic types of fires.
- Describe the proper use of the different types of fire extinguishers.
- Know your rights under the right-to-know laws.

Safety Notices

1. Explain the different meanings of *notes, cautions,* and *warnings* appearing in your textbook and engine manufacturer's manuals.

   _____

   _____

   _____

2. _____ _____ is the number one consideration when working with diesel engines.

   2. _____

Personal Safety

3. What are the advantages of keeping yourself and your uniform neat and clean?

_____

_____

_____

4. What is the danger in wearing loose clothing and jewelry when working in the shop?

_____

5. The most important part of the diesel technician's attire is _____.

5. _____

6. Technician A says diesel fuel is not volatile and there is no danger of diesel fuel flashing and burning around an open flame. Technician B says respiratory protection must always be worn when around solvent cleaning tanks and steam cleaners. Who is correct?

6. _____

   (A) A only.
   (B) B only.
   (C) Both A & B.
   (D) Neither A nor B.

7. Name four types of personal protection.

_____

_____

_____

_____

8. Jobs such as welding, chiseling, and grinding require that _____ be worn for adequate eye protection.

8. _____

9. Dust that contains _____, a known carcinogen, is potentially dangerous if respiratory protection is not worn.

9. _____

10. Technician A states that prolonged bare skin exposure to mild solvents is acceptable shop practice if hands are washed after contact. Technician B says it is best to wear earplugs when using pneumatic tools. Who is correct?

10. _____

   (A) A only.
   (B) B only.
   (C) Both A & B.
   (D) Neither A nor B.

Name _____

Shop Safety Rules

11. Describe proper lifting techniques for heavy objects.

_____

_____

12. What are the advantages to maintaining a clean work area?

_____

_____

13. What is the proper method of storing oily rags prior to disposal?

_____

14. Technician A says more accidents are caused by the improper use of power tools rather than hand tools. Technician B says technicians should clean all hand tools before returning them to their storage cabinet. Who is correct?

    (A) A only.
    (B) B only.
    (C) Both A & B.
    (D) Neither A nor B.

14. _____

15. Which of the following can be used to support vehicles off the ground?

    (A) Properly rated lifts with safety pins in place.
    (B) Properly rated jack stands.
    (C) Proper capacity crane lifts.
    (D) Both A & B.

15. _____

16. If the shop is not properly ventilated, a running engine can cause deadly _____ _____ to build up.

16. _____

17. In a diesel engine, diesel fuel may be under very high _____ and can penetrate the skin if connections are improperly opened.

17. _____

18. When using a starting aid in cold weather, which of the following should be done?

    (A) Prime the engine while it is cranked.
    (B) Use with glow plugs simultaneously.
    (C) Keep it away from spark and flame.
    (D) All of the above.

18. _____

19. Name three characteristics of cleaning solvents that can make working with them potentially dangerous.

_____

_____

_____

20. The makers of cleaning solvents and other potentially dangerous chemicals list handling precautions on

_____ _____ _____.

20. _____

21. Technician A uses kerosene to clean greased bearings. Technician B mixes different chemicals in fireproof containers prior to disposal. Who is correct?

    (A) A only.
    (B) B only.
    (C) Both A & B.
    (D) Neither A nor B.

21. _____

22. _____ _____ are typically placed on containers that hold potentially harmful materials.

22. _____

Fire Prevention

23. Name four different classes of fires that can occur in a diesel repair shop and the type of combustible materials involved.

_____

_____

_____

_____

24. Technician A uses a water or foam extinguisher on a small electrical fire. Technician B uses a foam extinguisher to douse an oil fire. Who is correct?

    (A) A only.
    (B) B only.
    (C) Both A & B.
    (D) Neither A nor B.

24. _____

Name _____

25. When using a foam extinguisher, Technician A allows the foam to fall lightly onto the fire. Technician B directs the stream of a carbon dioxide extinguisher as close to the flame as possible. Who is correct?
    (A) A only.
    (B) B only.
    (C) Both A & B.
    (D) Neither A nor B.

25. _____

Right-to-Know Laws

26. Name three types of information listed on Safety Data Sheets.

_____

_____

_____

27. Name the three major areas of employer responsibility to ensure a safe work area as outlined by OSHA.

_____

_____

_____

28. Name five materials commonly used in a diesel engine shop that are considered hazardous.

_____

_____

_____

_____

_____

29. When is a material considered to be hazardous waste?
    (A) When the shop is ready to dispose of it.
    (B) When it is removed from the vehicle.
    (C) When it becomes contaminated.
    (D) When it enters the shop.

29. _____

30. Waste oil, cleaning solvents, and antifreeze are all materials that can be _____ as a means of reducing the amount of waste that must be disposed.

30. _____

Name _____

Date _____

Instructor _____

Score _____ Text pages 37–60

Chapter 3

Tools, Precision Tools, and Fasteners

After studying this chapter and completing supplemental exercises, you will be able to:

- Describe the proper use of hand tools.
- Describe how to operate portable and stationary tools safely.
- Explain how to use a torque wrench.
- Explain how to use a micrometer.
- Name the different types of gauges used to take precision measurements.
- Understand the purpose of the various diesel injection system tools and measuring devices.
- Define the difference between U.S. customary and metric fasteners.

Hand Tools

1. Technician A says that most jobs can be safely completed using any one of several hand tools. Technician B states that hand tools cause fewer accidents than power tools. Who is correct?

(A) A only.

(B) B only.

(C) Both A & B.

(D) Neither A nor B.

1. _____

2. Why is it important to keep hand tools free of oil and grease?

3. The proper tool for cutting off damaged or badly rusted nuts, bolts, and rivet heads is a(n) _____.

3. _____

4. What is the proper way to hold a chisel?

   (A) Firmly and tightly just below the head.

   (B) Firmly and tightly in the midsection.

   (C) Steadily but loosely just below the head.

   (D) Steadily but loosely in the midsection.

4. _____

5. The brittleness of chisels and punches makes them a dangerous choice for _____.

   (A) cutting

   (B) driving out rivets

   (C) prying

   (D) All of the above.

5. _____

6. A(n) _____ is the most frequently used type of saw in a diesel shop.

6. _____

7. Why is it important to keep a saw sharp?

_____

8. When handling a knife, which of the following techniques is incorrect?

   (A) Keep handles clean and dry.

   (B) Complete the cut slowly.

   (C) Grip the tool firmly.

   (D) Cut toward your body.

8. _____

9. Identify the types of files shown in the illustration.

   (A) _____

   (B) _____

   (C) _____

   (D) _____

   (E) _____

10. Name three jobs for which a screwdriver should never be used.

_____

_____

_____

Name _____

11. When using a screwdriver, Technician A uses his
free hand to hold the tip of the tool in the screw slot
as he applies pressure. Technician B keeps the tip
perpendicular to the screw slot. Who is correct?

    (A) A only.

    (B) B only.

    (C) Both A & B.

    (D) Neither A nor B.

11. _____

12. A screwdriver with a(n) _____ handle is best for
electrical work.

12. _____

13. The following type of hammer is filled with metal
shot to reduce rebound as it strikes an object.

    (A) Dead blow.

    (B) Sledge.

    (C) Ball peen.

    (D) None of the above.

13. _____

14. Technician A grips the handle of a hammer near the
bottom to generate more leverage. Technician B
keeps the hammer parallel to the work to distribute
the striking force over the entire face of the hammer.
Who is correct?

    (A) A only.

    (B) B only.

    (C) Both A & B.

    (D) Neither A nor B.

14. _____

15. Name two types of wrenches designed to be used in a tight place.

    _____

    _____

16. A(n) _____ is the most commonly used type of socket
handle.

16. _____

17. When using a socket wrench, Technician A keeps the
ratchet as close to the socket as possible. Technician B
always pulls the handle toward herself when loosening
or tightening a bolt. Who is correct?

    (A) A only.

    (B) B only.

    (C) Both A & B.

    (D) Neither A nor B.

17. _____

18. This type of wrench can fit onto a ratchet or breaker for high torque applications.

    (A) Open end.

    (B) Allen socket.

    (C) Flare nut.

    (D) None of the above.

18. _____

19. Technician A replaces worn Allen head wrenches on a regular basis. Technician B uses an impact wrench to loosen a stubborn Allen head bolt. Who is correct?

    (A) A only.

    (B) B only.

    (C) Both A & B.

    (D) Neither A nor B.

19. _____

20. Identify the various types of pliers shown.

    (A) _____ (F) _____

    (B) _____ (G) _____

    (C) _____ (H) _____

    (D) _____ (I) _____

    (E) _____

Name _____

21. Technician A uses diagonal cutting pliers to cut through   21. _____
    a wire. Technician B uses pliers to loosen a bolt. Who
    is correct?
    (A) A only.
    (B) B only.
    (C) Both A & B.
    (D) Neither A nor B.

22. Name three designs of torque wrenches.

    _____

    _____

    _____

23. Handle extensions should not be used with which type   23. _____
    of torque wrench?
    (A) Snap or click.
    (B) Dial.
    (C) Beam.
    (D) Both A & B.

24. Why is it important to apply steady pressure when using a torque wrench?

    _____

    _____

25. _____ measurement ensures like fasteners will exert   25. _____
    the same amount of force without deviation from one
    fastener to the next.
    (A) Torque
    (B) Torque/angle
    (C) Torque/compression
    (D) All of the above.

26. Name the two basic types of puller hand tools used in diesel work.

    _____

    _____

Power Tools

27. Name the two ways power tools can be driven.

    _____

    _____

28. Another name for an air tool is a(n) _____ tool.   28. _____

29. List four advantages of air-powered tools over electric power tools.

_____

_____

_____

_____

30. List five safety rules for operating stationary power tools.

_____

_____

_____

_____

_____

31. When using a drill press, always use a(n) _____ _____   31. _____
    to start the drill bit.

32. The following type of grinder is the one most   32. _____
    frequently used in a diesel shop.
    (A) Surface.
    (B) Bench.
    (C) Flywheel.
    (D) None of the above.

33. Why is it best to avoid grinding aluminum or brass with an abrasive stone?

_____

34. When working on a hydraulic press, position yourself   34. _____
    _____.
    (A) in front of the press
    (B) in back of the press
    (C) to the side of the press
    (D) Either A or B.

35. Name three types of welding equipment typically used in a diesel engine shop.

_____

_____

_____

Name _____

Engine Measuring Tools

36. Technician A makes all precision measurements with the tool and part at room temperature. Technician B calibrates all shop micrometers on a regular basis. Who is correct?

    (A) A only.

    (B) B only.

    (C) Both A & B.

    (D) Neither A nor B.

36. _____

37. Name two types of standard and metric micrometers.

    _____

    _____

38. Each complete turn of the thimble on a micrometer moves the spindle _____.

    (A) .010″

    (B) .025″

    (C) .035″

    (D) .050″

38. _____

39. What is the reading on the 1″ to 2″ micrometer shown here?

    _____

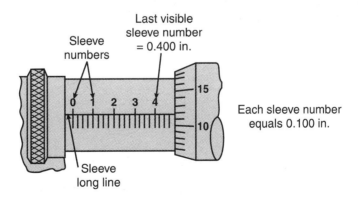

40. Which tool is used to measure the difference between parallel surfaces of a part and a recess in that part?

    (A) Inside micrometer.

    (B) Outside micrometer.

    (C) Depth gauge.

    (D) Telescoping or snap gauge.

40. _____

41. A vernier caliper can be used for which of the following measurements?

    (A) Inside.

    (B) Outside.

    (C) Depth.

    (D) All of the above.

41. _____

42. Which tool is used to measure bore diameters?

    (A) Feeler gauge.

    (B) Outside micrometer.

    (C) Telescoping or snap gauge.

    (D) Depth gauge.

42. _____

43. The _____ _____ gauge is used to measure holes that are too small for a snap gauge.

43. _____

44. List four job uses for a dial indicator.

    _____

    _____

    _____

    _____

45. Using a(n) _____ _____ allows an accurate and safe way for the technician to determine a diesel engine's speed.

45. _____

46. The following thermometer is designed to measure temperature from a distance, reducing the potential risk of injury for the technician.

    (A) Laser.

    (B) Digital.

    (C) Infrared.

    (D) None of the above.

46. _____

47. The most reliable method of measuring cylinder load is to measure the firing pressure using a(n) _____ _____.

47. _____

48. A water or mercury manometer can be used to check _____ _____ and restriction in the intake and exhaust systems.

48. _____

Name _____

Specialized Diesel Tools and Equipment

49. Technician A states that some fuel injectors are press fit into the cylinder block and may require a special injector extractor. Technician B says an injector puller provides a grip on the injector body when clearance between the valve springs is limited. Who is correct?

    (A) A only.
    (B) B only.
    (C) Both A & B.
    (D) Neither A nor B.

49. _____

50. A(n) _____ uses a set of pressure gauges and valves to measure injector pump operation.

    (A) injection pump tester
    (B) nozzle pop tester
    (C) injector service set
    (D) manometer tester

50. _____

51. List four tests or conditions that can be verified using an injector pop-n-fixture tester.

    _____

    _____

    _____

    _____

52. A comparison of _____ _____ resistance may indicate that one or more cylinders is not firing properly.

52. _____

53. Diesel engine exhaust quality is expressed in terms of the exhaust smoke's _____.

53. _____

Electrical Test Equipment

54. Multimeters with _____ readout displays are preferred in electrical test work because they give fast, precise readings.

54. _____

55. Technician A says self-powered test lights can be used to determine continuity in a circuit. Technician B says self-powered test lights should not be used on solid state circuitry. Who is correct?
    (A) A only.
    (B) B only.
    (C) Both A & B.
    (D) Neither A nor B.

55. _____

56. _____ _____ are used to temporarily bypass circuits or circuit components for electrical testing.

56. _____

Computer System Diagnostic Tools

57. The most common diagnostic tool for computerized engine control systems is a handheld or portable _____ _____.

57. _____

58. Electronic diagnostic tools connect to the engine's computer via a(n) _____ _____ _____.

58. _____

59. Technician A states that personal and laptop computers can now run software programs that help diagnose engine problems. Technician B states that these programs can also be used to program customer specific engine parameters and other operating data. Who is correct?
    (A) A only.
    (B) B only.
    (C) Both A & B.
    (D) Neither A nor B.

59. _____

Name _____

Fasteners
---

60. Name five different identifying characteristics of bolts and screws used in diesel engines.

   _____

   _____

   _____

   _____

   _____

61. Name the two measuring systems used for bolts and screws.

   _____

   _____

62. Technician A says that certain sizes of metric and USC   62. _____
   bolts and nuts are interchangeable. Technician B says
   that thread pitch is measured differently in the USC
   and metric systems. Who is correct?

   (A) A only.

   (B) B only.

   (C) Both A & B.

   (D) Neither A nor B.

63. Label the three major characteristics shown on the bolt illustrated. The USC system is being used.

   (A) _____

   (B) _____

   (C) _____

64. The amount of stress or stretch a bolt is able to   64. _____
   withstand is measured by its _____ _____.

65. What does the letter *L* stamped on a bolt indicate?

   _____

Thread Repairs

66. A(n) _____ and _____ set can be used to repair stripped threads.

66. _____

67. Technician A says that the plating on a bolt can act as a lubricant, making it easier to over-torque. Technician B says most torque-to-yield fasteners can be reused. Who is correct?

    (A) A only.

    (B) B only.

    (C) Both A & B.

    (D) Neither A nor B.

67. _____

68. Fasteners designed to be torqued barely into a yield condition are called _____-_____-_____ fasteners.

68. _____

69. Technician A says most printed torque valves are for dry, plated bolts. Technician B says greasy or oily fingers do not provide sufficient lubricant to a bolt to affect its torque value. Who is correct?

    (A) A only.

    (B) B only.

    (C) Both A & B.

    (D) Neither A nor B.

69. _____

Name _____

Date _____

Instructor _____

Score _____ Text pages 61–86

Chapter 4

Principles of Engine Operation

After studying this chapter and completing supplemental exercises, you will be able to:

- Explain the operating principles and interaction of the major diesel engine components, such as the cylinder block, cylinder head, valve train, and accessory items.
- Explain the difference between two-stroke cycle and four-stroke cycle diesel engines and describe what happens during each piston stroke in both types.
- Explain the basics of both two-cycle and four-cycle valve timing.
- Define the most popular diesel engine configurations.
- Name the two types of combustion chamber designs.
- Explain the difference between direct and indirect fuel injection.
- List the functions of the fuel injection system and name the five types of fuel injection systems used in modern diesel engines.
- Explain the basic engine performance terms and formulas, such as bore, stroke, compression ratio, volumetric efficiency, horsepower, and torque.

Major Engine Components

1. All of the parts located above the engine's cylinder block are commonly referred to as the _____ _____.

2. Joined engine surfaces must be perfectly sealed with _____ designed to withstand the temperature and pressures generated inside the engine.

1. _____

2. _____

3. The _____ _____ supports all major engine
   components and is the foundation of the diesel engine.

3. _____

4. Name the two types of cylinder liners used in diesel engines.

_____

_____

5. Identify the components in this cross-section illustration of a wet liner cylinder block.

   (A) _____

   (B) _____

   (C) _____

   (D) _____

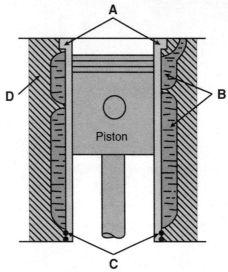

Piston

6. A(n) _____ _____ is a passage in the cylinder block
   that allows coolant to move around the outside of the
   cylinder and carry off the intense heat generated by
   combustion.

6. _____

7. The _____ acts as a movable seal that forms the
   bottom of the combustion chamber.

7. _____

8. Grooves cut into the surface of the piston are fitted
   with _____ _____ that seal in the compression and
   combustion pressure and also control the lubricating
   oil film on the wall of the cylinder liner.

8. _____

9. Describe the main functions of the top, middle, and bottom piston rings.

   Top ring: _____

   Middle ring: _____

   Bottom ring: _____

Name _____

10. The _____ converts the reciprocal (up-and-down) motion of the pistons into rotary (turning) motion.

10. _____

11. _____ _____ are installed at the points the crankshaft passes through the front and rear walls of the cylinder block.

11. _____

12. _____ are the sections of the crankshaft that ride in the cylinder block saddles.

12. _____

13. Connecting rod journals are located at the ends of the _____ _____.

13. _____

14. Drilled passages in the crankshaft are known as _____ _____.

14. _____

15. _____ gears are mounted on the crankshaft and camshaft of a diesel engine.

15. _____

16. What forms the link between the piston and the crankshaft?

16. _____

(A) Journal.

(B) Connecting rod.

(C) Wrist pin.

(D) Flywheel.

17. The _____ _____ forms the bottom of the engine.

17. _____

18. The _____ is used to store some of the kinetic energy of the power stroke to help smooth out crankshaft motion.

18. _____

19. Torsional harmonics (lengthwise twisting) in an engine is eliminated through the use of a(n) _____.

19. _____

(A) vibration damper

(B) internal balancer

(C) flywheel

(D) Both A and B.

20. The _____ coordinates the operation of the intake and exhaust valves (and in some fuel injection systems, the fuel injectors) with the action of the pistons.

20. _____

21. The cam lobes of the camshaft are _____ in shape.

21. _____

(A) round

(B) eccentric

(C) parabolic

(D) elliptical

22. To synchronize the action of the valves and injectors   22. _____
with the movement of the pistons, _____ _____ on the
camshaft and crankshaft are meshed and timed.

23. Identify the following valve train components.

(A) _____

(B) _____

(C) _____

(D) _____

(E) _____

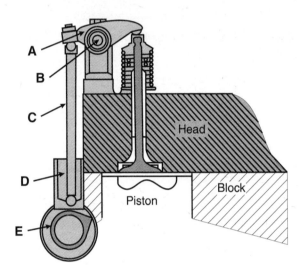

24. _____, also called lifters or tappets, convert the   24. _____
rotational motion of the cam lobe into a reciprocating
motion.

(A) Rocker arms

(B) Cam followers

(C) Push tubes

(D) Lobe tubes

25. The _____ connect the cam followers to the rocker   25. _____
arms.

(A) timing gears

(B) cam rockers

(C) push tubes

(D) lobe tubes

Name _____

26. The _____ is a large casting that bolts to the cylinder block and forms the top of the combustion chamber.
    (A) valve train
    (B) blower
    (C) turbocharger
    (D) cylinder head

26. _____

27. The _____ _____ is installed between the cylinder head and the cylinder block.

27. _____

28. _____ are used to seal the air passages in the cylinder.

28. _____

29. Diesel engine valves may be filled with _____ to help transfer heat to the top of the valve.
    (A) Stellite
    (B) water
    (C) sodium
    (D) copper

29. _____

30. To ensure a very tight valve seal, most modern, high-powered diesel engines use a separate _____ _____ inserted into the cylinder head.

30. _____

31. When two valves are used for the same function in a cylinder, a(n) _____ is added to form a bridge between the two valves.

31. _____

32. Name the two types of manifolds used on a diesel engine.

_____

_____

33. Because they are subject to rapid and extreme variations in temperature, exhaust manifolds are normally manufactured from _____.
    (A) stainless steel
    (B) cast iron
    (C) aluminum
    (D) copper

33. _____

34. A(n) _____ is an air pump that is mechanically driven by the engine to force more air into the combustion chamber.

34. _____

35. Technician A says turbochargers are more widely used on four-cycle diesel engines than superchargers. Technician B says because they are driven by the engine's exhaust gas, turbochargers work at one rated level. Who is correct?

    (A) A only.

    (B) B only.

    (C) Both A & B.

    (D) Neither A nor B.

35. _____

36. Turbochargers can increase engine power by up to _____ on small diesel engines.

    (A) 10%

    (B) 25%

    (C) 40%

    (D) 50%

36. _____

37. A charge air cooler is simply a radiator that is used to cool _____.

    (A) engine coolant

    (B) diesel fuel

    (C) oil

    (D) intake air

37. _____

38. What is the advantage of cooling intake air before it enters the cylinder?

    _____

Diesel Engine Classifications

39. Name five ways of classifying diesel engines.

    _____

    _____

    _____

    _____

    _____

40. A four-cycle engine requires _____ full turn(s) of the crankshaft to complete the combustion cycle.

    (A) one

    (B) two

    (C) four

    (D) two or four

40. _____

Name _____

41. Name the four strokes of a four-cycle engine.

_____

_____

_____

_____

42. During the _____ stroke, the piston is near the top of   42. _____
the cylinder, the intake valve is open, and the exhaust
valve is closed.

43. During the _____ stroke, both the intake and exhaust   43. _____
valves are closed on a four-cycle engine.

44. On a four-cycle diesel engine, the length of the power   44. _____
stroke is controlled by the amount of time the _____
valves remain closed.

45. On a four-cycle diesel engine, name two ways the exhaust gases are removed from the
cylinder.

_____

_____

46. In relation to engine timing, what do the following abbreviations stand for?

TDC: _____

BDC: _____

ATDC: _____

BBDC: _____

47. A two-cycle engine requires _____ full turn(s) of the   47. _____
    crankshaft to complete the combustion cycle.
    (A) one
    (B) two
    (C) four
    (D) two or four

48. On a two-cycle diesel engine, separate intake and   48. _____
    exhaust strokes are _____.

49. Intake ports of a two-cycle engine are open when the   49. _____
    piston is at the _____ of its stroke.

50. Explain what scavenging is and how it occurs in two-stroke cycle engines.

    _____

    _____

51. On a two-cycle or stroke engine, the _____ supplies a   51. _____
    strong flow of air into the cylinder whenever the intake
    ports are not blocked by the piston.

52. Intake occurs as part of the _____ stroke in a two-cycle   52. _____
    engine.

53. In a two-stroke engine, the power stroke continues   53. _____
    until the piston _____.
    (A) reaches TDC
    (B) reaches BDC
    (C) is about halfway down the cylinder
    (D) None of the above.

54. On a two-cycle engine, intake ports normally open   54. _____
    around 60° BBDC on the power stroke and remain
    open around _____ ABDC on the compression stroke.
    (A) 30°
    (B) 45°
    (C) 60°
    (D) 90°

Cylinder Number and Configuration

55. List three advantages of an inline engine configuration.

    _____

    _____

Name _____

56. List two advantages of a V-type engine configuration.

_____

_____

57. W-cylinder engine arrangements are used primarily in _____.
    (A) locomotives
    (B) marine applications
    (C) industrial applications
    (D) mobile off-highway vehicles

57. _____

58. Delta cylinder engine arrangements are used primarily in _____.
    (A) locomotives
    (B) passenger vehicles
    (C) industrial applications
    (D) mobile off-highway vehicles

58. _____

59. In a(n) _____ engine configuration, the cylinders are arranged in a circle around a common crankshaft.
    (A) delta
    (B) double-acting
    (C) radial
    (D) V-type

59. _____

60. A(n) _____ engine configuration is most common on very large, low-speed engines.
    (A) delta
    (B) double-acting piston
    (C) radial
    (D) V-type

60. _____

Combustion Chamber Designs

61. Name four types of combustion chambers.

_____

_____

_____

_____

62. List two major advantages of direct injection.

_____

_____

63. Technician A states that precombustion chamber diesel engines produce smooth, quiet combustion. Technician B states that reduced fuel consumption is the main advantage of these indirect injection systems. Who is correct?

    (A) A only.
    (B) B only.
    (C) Both A & B.
    (D) Neither A nor B.

63. _____

64. Which type of combustion chamber uses an auxiliary chamber with a throat area that opens at an angle to the main combustion chamber?

    (A) Energy cell.
    (B) Swirl.
    (C) Direct.
    (D) Precombustion.

64. _____

65. Which type of combustion chamber is generally used with pintle-type injection nozzles?

    (A) Energy cell.
    (B) Swirl.
    (C) Direct.
    (D) Precombustion.

65. _____

Diesel Fuel Injection Systems

66. What is the most common problem caused when fuel is injected into the combustion chamber at the wrong time?

    (A) Loss of power.
    (B) White exhaust smoke.
    (C) Rough idling.
    (D) Stalling.

66. _____

Name _____

67. Technician A says slight variations in the amount of
fuel delivered to each cylinder can cause a rough
running engine. Technician B says if the fuel is injected
too early, ignition will be delayed and combustion will
be incomplete. Who is correct?

    (A) A only.

    (B) B only.

    (C) Both A & B.

    (D) Neither A nor B.

67. _____

68. What is *atomization* and why is it important in fuel injection?

_____

_____

69. The _____ regulates the amount of fuel fed to diesel
engine cylinders.

    (A) distributor

    (B) governor

    (C) fuel pump

    (D) energy cell

69. _____

70. List the seven major types of diesel fuel injection systems.

_____

_____

_____

_____

_____

_____

_____

71. _____ fuel injection systems are only used on slow-
speed industrial or marine engines.

    (A) Individual pump per cylinder

    (B) Unit injector

    (C) Distributor pump

    (D) Multiple-plunger, inline pump

71. _____

72. The _____ uses individual pumps that are contained
within a single injection pump housing.

    (A) individual pump per cylinder

    (B) unit injector

    (C) distributor pump

    (D) multiple-plunger, inline pump

72. _____

73. In a(n) _____ fuel system, timing, atomization, metering, and fuel pressure generation all take place inside the injector body that serves a particular cylinder.

    (A) pressure-time

    (B) unit injectors

    (C) distributor pumps

    (D) multiple-plunger, inline pump

73. _____

74. Which type of fuel injection system can generate the highest fuel pressures?

    (A) Pressure-time.

    (B) Unit injectors.

    (C) Distributor pumps.

    (D) Multiple-plunger, inline pump.

74. _____

75. In a PT injection system, which factor affects the amount of fuel injected into the combustion chamber?

    (A) Fuel pressure.

    (B) The time the injector is open.

    (C) The size of the injector orifice.

    (D) All of the above.

75. _____

76. _____ fuel injection systems are used on small to medium engines.

    (A) Pressure-time

    (B) Unit injector

    (C) Distributor pump

    (D) Multiple-plunger inline pump

76. _____

77. Increasingly stringent exhaust emission standards for diesel powered vehicles led to the development of _____ over the past ten to fifteen years.

    (A) puff limiters

    (B) unit injection systems

    (C) electronic engine control systems

    (D) lean diesel fuels

77. _____

Name _____

Engine Performance Terms and Formulas

78. The diameter of a cylinder is called the cylinder _____.

    (A) width

    (B) bore

    (C) displacement

    (D) capacity

78. _____

79. The distance a piston travels between its top dead center and bottom dead center positions is known as _____.

    (A) displacement

    (B) stroke

    (C) lash

    (D) bore

79. _____

80. The total volume that is placed in a cylinder as the piston moves from the bottom to the top is _____.

    (A) engine displacement

    (B) volumetric efficiency

    (C) cylinder displacement

    (D) compression ratio

80. _____

81. The amount of compression developed in a cylinder is expressed by the _____.

    (A) engine displacement

    (B) volumetric efficiency

    (C) mean effective pressure

    (D) compression ratio

81. _____

82. Technician A says atmospheric pressures are less at higher altitudes and can cause engine operating problems. Technician B says atmospheric pressure at sea level is 100 psi. Who is correct?

    (A) A only.

    (B) B only.

    (C) Both A & B.

    (D) Neither A nor B.

82. _____

83. The amount of air that is actually pulled into a diesel engine cylinder compared to the total volume that could theoretically fill the cylinder is known as the _____.

    (A) engine displacement
    (B) volumetric efficiency
    (C) mean effective pressure
    (D) compression ratio

83. _____

84. _____ _____ compares the weight of a material with the weight of an equal volume of water.

84. _____

85. _____ is the difference between the compression pressure and the expansion pressure in an engine.

    (A) Engine displacement
    (B) Volumetric efficiency
    (C) Mean effective pressure
    (D) Compression ratio

85. _____

Horsepower and Torque

Items 86 through 88. Match the term with the definition.

    (A) Brake horsepower
    (B) Indicated horsepower
    (C) Rated horsepower

86. Produced by an engine at its maximum full-load, governed speed.

86. _____

87. Transmitted to the pistons by combustion gases.

87. _____

88. Usable horsepower produced by engine.

88. _____

89. The rotational or twisting force around a fixed point is known as _____.

    (A) centrifugal force
    (B) deflective power
    (C) torque
    (D) vector force

89. _____

90. Torque is measured in _____.

    (A) foot-pounds
    (B) inch-pounds
    (C) Newton-meters
    (D) All of the above.

90. _____

Name _____

Date _____

Instructor _____

Score _____ Text pages 87–108

Chapter 5

Engine Blocks

After studying this chapter and completing supplemental exercises, you will be able to:

- Explain how to gain access to the components in a stationary engine.
- Explain how to remove a mobile engine from its installation.
- Describe how to remove the basic parts from a mobile diesel engine block.
- Name two popular methods used to clean engine blocks.
- Conduct a cylinder block inspection.
- Inspect a cylinder and liner.
- Name the two types of cylinder liners.
- Describe how to install a cylinder liner.

Cylinder Blocks

1. The _____ is the largest single component of the modern diesel engine.

1. _____

2. Welded cylinder block construction is used on what major classification of diesel engine?

   (A) Mobile.

   (B) Two-cycle.

   (C) Large stationary.

   (D) Four-cycle.

2. _____

3. One-piece cylinder block construction is used on what   3. _____
major classification of diesel engine?

   (A) Mobile.

   (B) Two-cycle.

   (C) Large stationary.

   (D) Four-cycle.

4. The drilled oil passages of a cylinder block are called   4. _____
_____.

Accessing Diesel Engine Components

5. The portion of the block that serves as a housing for   5. _____
the crankshaft is commonly called the _____.

6. On some very large engines, spring-loaded access   6. _____
covers called _____ _____ serve as safety devices to
release higher than normal engine pressures.

7. A(n) _____ is a device that controls the radiator shutters   7. _____
on a mobile diesel engine.

8. When removing a diesel engine from an on-highway   8. _____
truck, Technician A makes sure refrigerant from the
air-conditioning systems does not escape into the
atmosphere. Technician B lifts the engine out of the
truck using a strap under the oil pan. Who is correct?

   (A) A only.

   (B) B only.

   (C) Both A & B.

   (D) Neither A nor B.

9. When disassembling a mobile diesel engine,   9. _____
Technician A marks the rocker housings according to
their location before removing them. Technician B caps
the fuel injector opening to prevent dirt from entering
the cylinders. Who is correct?

   (A) A only.

   (B) B only.

   (C) Both A & B.

   (D) Neither A nor B.

Name _____

10. Technician A pries an engine oil pan off using a large screwdriver. Technician B locks the crankshaft in position before removing the flywheel bolts. Who is correct?

    (A) A only.

    (B) B only.

    (C) Both A & B.

    (D) Neither A nor B.

10. _____

11. Technician A removes the camshaft by rotating it while pulling it out of the block using steady pressure. When removing a piston and connecting rod assembly, Technician B positions the crankshaft throw for that assembly at the top of its stroke. Who is correct?

    (A) A only.

    (B) B only.

    (C) Both A & B.

    (D) Neither A nor B.

11. _____

12. After the connecting rod cap has been removed, cover the rod bolts with _____ to prevent damage to the crankshaft.

    (A) engine oil

    (B) journal protectors or lengths of vacuum hose

    (C) fluorescent penetrant

    (D) None of the above.

12. _____

13. After the crankshaft has been removed from the engine block, support the crankshaft using a(n) _____-_____ to prevent sag that could damage the shaft.

13. _____

14. The first step in cleaning an engine block is to remove all _____ _____ and freeze plugs.

14. _____

15. To remove a cup-type freeze plug, Technician A pulls it out with a slide hammer. Technician B drives it out from the back side using a long rod. Who is correct?

    (A) A only.

    (B) B only.

    (C) Both A & B.

    (D) Neither A nor B.

15. _____

16. What is the best method of removing a flat-type engine plug?

_____

17. What is the best method of removing threaded oil gallery plugs?

_____

18. Name two factors that can influence the method used to clean an engine block.

_____

_____

19. Name the two basic block cleaning procedures.

_____

_____

20. Hot alkaline tank cleaning is often used on blocks   20. _____
    made of _____ _____.

21. Emulsion-type cleaning solutions must be used on   21. _____
    components made of _____.

22. Once extremely popular, _____ cleaning of engine   22. _____
    blocks has been phased out due to environmental
    regulations.

23. Name two acceptable ways of removing the dry powdery ash left on parts cleaned in a
    thermal cleaning oven.

_____

_____

24. Which of the following methods can be used to check   24. _____
    the engine block for cracks?
    (A) Dye or powder testing.
    (B) Magnetic crack testing.
    (C) Visual inspection.
    (D) All of the above.

25. Technician A says some types of cracks in engine   25. _____
    blocks can be repaired. Technician B says that any
    cracks in the block require the block to be replaced.
    Who is correct?
    (A) A only.
    (B) B only.
    (C) Both A & B.
    (D) Neither A nor B.

Name _____

26. List five common areas for cracks and other engine block defects to occur.

   _____

   _____

   _____

   _____

   _____

27. List the three ways a cylinder block must be checked for deck warpage using a straightedge and feeler gauge.

   _____

   _____

   _____

28. _____ can be used to correct cylinder block deck warpage.

   (A) Grinding

   (B) Milling

   (C) Broaching

   (D) All of the above.

28. _____

29. The _____ _____ is the distance from the crankshaft centerline to the block deck.

29. _____

30. Technician A performs deck height measurements at both the front and rear of the engine block. Technician B says these measurements should not differ by more than .005″ (127 mm). Who is correct?

   (A) A only.

   (B) B only.

   (C) Both A & B.

   (D) Neither A nor B.

30. _____

31. Most diesel engine cylinder blocks are constructed with _____.

   (A) integral cylinder bores

   (B) enbloc bores

   (C) parent bores

   (D) replaceable cylinder bore sleeves

31. _____

32. Which of the following is a function of a cylinder liner?

   (A) Seal combustion pressure.

   (B) Transfer heat of combustion to the coolant.

   (C) Guide the path of the piston.

   (D) All of the above.

32. _____

33. A(n) _____-stroke diesel engine has cylinder liners that   33. _____
    contain air inlet ports.

34. Identify the parts of a diesel engine cylinder wet liner.

    (A) _____

    (B) _____

    (C) _____

    (D) _____

    (E) _____

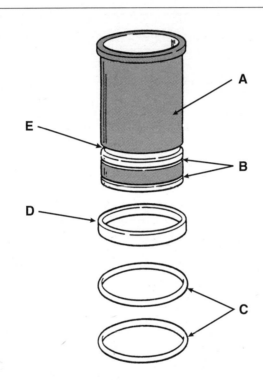

35. The material most commonly used in the construction   35. _____
    of cylinder liners is _____.

    (A) aluminum

    (B) stainless steel

    (C) close-grain cast iron

    (D) open-grain cast iron

36. Cylinder liners are normally plated on their wearing   36. _____
    surfaces with _____.

    (A) stainless steel

    (B) zinc

    (C) porous chromium

    (D) close-grain cast iron

Name _____

37. When the oil film between the piston and cylinder wall breaks down, what can occur?

    (A) Scoring.

    (B) Point welding.

    (C) Both of the above.

    (D) Neither of the above.

37. _____

38. Cylinder wear is _____.

    (A) most severe at the bottom of the cylinder

    (B) most severe at the top of the ring travel area

    (C) uniform along the entire cylinder

    (D) unpredictable from engine to engine

38. _____

39. What two tools can be used to check for cylinder wear or taper?

_____

_____

40. Whenever cylinder taper or out-of-roundness exceeds _____, the engine should be rebored or relined.

    (A) .0025″ (.0625 mm)

    (B) .005″ (.127 mm)

    (C) .075″ (.189 mm)

    (D) .010″ (.255 mm)

40. _____

41. In a worn cylinder liner, a(n) _____ often is found near the top of the piston ring travel zone.

41. _____

42. A(n) _____ _____ is used to remove ridges from the cylinder liner.

42. _____

43. The _____ of the cylinder liner rests on the counterbore machined into the top of the bore.

43. _____

44. The depth of a block counterbore should not vary more than _____ around the entire counterbore.

    (A) .001″ (.0254 mm)

    (B) .002″ (.050 mm)

    (C) .003″ (.075 mm)

    (D) .004″ (1.00 mm)

44. _____

45. Technician A says that when a cylinder liner is worn beyond acceptable limits, the piston is also worn and should be replaced. Technician B says a reconditioned counterbore must have a chamfer on its inside diameter. Who is correct?

45. _____

(A) A only.

(B) B only.

(C) Both A & B.

(D) Neither A nor B.

46. Name the two types of cylinder liners.

_____

_____

47. Identify the parts of a dry cylinder liner.

(A) _____   (F) _____

(B) _____   (G) _____

(C) _____   (H) _____

(D) _____   (I) _____

(E) _____   (J) _____

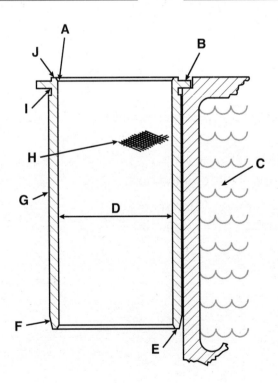

Name _____

48. Identify the parts of a wet cylinder liner.

(A) _____   (L) _____

(B) _____   (M) _____

(C) _____   (N) _____

(D) _____   (O) _____

(E) _____   (P) _____

(F) _____   (Q) _____

(G) _____   (R) _____

(H) _____   (S) _____

(I) _____   (T) _____

(J) _____   (U) _____

(K) _____   (V) _____

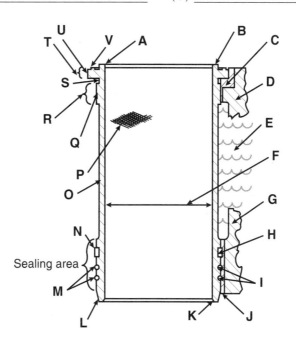

49. Dry cylinder liners _____.   49. _____

    (A) are generally used in large diesel engines

    (B) are usually thicker than wet liners

    (C) can be installed using a press fit or loose fit

    (D) All of the above.

50. A critical seal is formed on a wet cylinder liner by the   50. _____
top flange and _____.
   (A) air inlet ports
   (B) bottom sealing rings
   (C) barrel
   (D) None of the above.

51. Rubber or neoprene sealing rings around the bottom of   51. _____
the wet liner prevent engine coolant from leaking into
the _____ _____.

52. Name three reasons a cylinder liner should be removed and replaced.

   _____

   _____

   _____

53. A cylinder liner can be gripped and removed from an   53. _____
engine block using a special hand- or hydraulic-
powered tool called a(n) _____ _____ _____.

54. _____ the cylinder is vitally important in obtaining   54. _____
proper piston ring seating.

55. After honing, _____ should be used to clean the   55. _____
cylinder walls.
   (A) kerosene
   (B) diesel fuel
   (C) laundry detergent
   (D) solvent

56. After cleaning the honed cylinder, it should be rubbed   56. _____
with _____ and a clean cloth to remove all remaining
debris.
   (A) engine oil
   (B) diesel fuel
   (C) gasoline
   (D) WD-40

57. On smaller engine blocks, _____ can be used in place   57. _____
of reboring if the diameter of the bore is not altered.
   (A) honing
   (B) deglazing
   (C) buffing
   (D) sanding

Name _____

58. Technician A says it is best to remove the crankshaft
    from the block before deglazing. Technician B uses
    a slow spinning drill (300–500 rpm) to drive the
    deglazing tool. Who is correct?

    (A) A only.

    (B) B only.

    (C) Both A & B.

    (D) Neither A nor B.

58. _____

59. What procedure is shown in the illustration?

_____

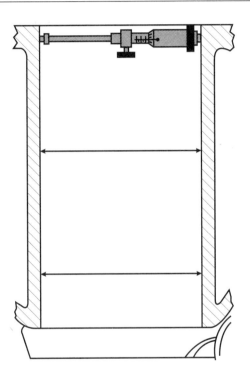

60. When properly installed, a press-fit dry cylinder liner
    will _____.

    (A) extend slightly above the deck of the block

    (B) sit slightly below the deck of the block

    (C) sit flush with the deck of the block

    (D) extend two inches into the oil pan

60. _____

61. An accumulation of carbon deposits on the liner's
    outside diameter and pronounced dark areas are signs
    the liner _____.

    (A) is installed too loosely

    (B) is installed too tightly

    (C) is not properly honed

    (D) is properly installed above the cylinder deck

61. _____

62. Block distortion, liner collapse, hot spots, and scuffing are common problems when the liner _____.
    (A) is installed too loosely
    (B) is installed too tightly
    (C) is not properly honed
    (D) is properly installed above the cylinder deck

62. _____

63. On liner O-rings, the parting line on the ring should be _____ the groove when the seal is properly installed.
    (A) slightly above
    (B) slightly below
    (C) parallel to
    (D) perpendicular to

63. _____

64. A(n) _____ can be used to remove twists in cylinder liner seals during installation.
    (A) straightedge
    (B) wrench
    (C) small screwdriver
    (D) seal edger

64. _____

65. After the cylinder liner is properly installed in the block, clean the flange using a(n) _____ to ensure proper measurement of the flange height above the block.
    (A) stainless steel pad
    (B) brass wire brush or pad
    (C) strong solvent
    (D) belt sander

65. _____

66. If a cylinder block deck is resurfaced, the cylinder block _____ depth must be recut to specifications.

66. _____

67. _____ can be used to re-establish the correct liner flange height.

67. _____

68. A liner flange may contain a(n) _____ to protect the head gasket from the direct impact of combustion.

68. _____

69. _____ beads are often machined into liner flanges to promote sealing between the liner and the head gasket.

69. _____

Name _____

Date_____

Instructor_____

Score_____ Text pages 109–130

Chapter 6
Crankshafts

After studying this chapter and completing supplemental exercises, you will be able to:

- Explain the purpose of a crankshaft.
- Recognize common crankshaft terminology.
- Describe the various crankshaft classifications.
- Inspect a crankshaft for defects.
- Describe methods used to recondition a crankshaft.
- Describe the purpose of the flywheel and vibration damper.

Diesel Crankshafts

1. The _____ _____ _____ serve as the crankshaft's center of rotation and primary means of support.

1. _____

2. In order that longer-wearing, more durable bearing metal can be used without causing excessive wear of the bearings, journal surfaces are _____.

2. _____

3. The section of the crankshaft that consists of two webs and a connecting rod journal is referred to as a(n) _____.

3. _____

4. To reduce weight and provide a passage for the flow of lubricating oil, the rod and main journals of a crankshaft may be _____.

4. _____

5. To balance the off-center weight of the individual throws and keep the centrifugal force generated by each in equilibrium, part of the web extends beyond the main journal to form or support _____.

5. _____

6. Combustion forces in a diesel engine are produced and transmitted to the crankshaft in a pulsating manner that creates "twisting" vibrations referred to as _____ vibrations.

6. _____

7. Lubricating oil under pressure enters the main bearings and is forced through diagonal passages in the crankshaft to the _____ bearings.

7. _____

8. When diesel engines use connecting rods with drilled passages to carry lubricating oil from the rod bearings to the other end of the rods, the oil being pumped through the rod is being used for pin lubrication and

_____ _____.

8. _____

9. Crankshafts are generally classified by the number of _____ bearings.
   (A) rod
   (B) main
   (C) Both rod and main.
   (D) None of the above.

9. _____

10. A V-block engine will have _____ main bearings than an inline engine with the same number of cylinders.
    (A) more
    (B) less
    (C) the same
    (D) Any of the above.

10. _____

11. When storing a crankshaft that has been removed from an engine, it is important to make sure the crankshaft has proper support along its entire length to prevent

_____.

11. _____

12. When visually inspecting a crankshaft, discoloration of the journals may be evident. What is the usual cause of this discoloration when induction hardening is not used on the crankshaft?
    (A) Excessive wear.
    (B) Stress fatigue.
    (C) Excessive heat.
    (D) Torsional vibration.

12. _____

Name _____

13. The purpose of subjecting a crankshaft to a magnetic
particle test is to _____.

    (A) check for flaws, such as cracks

    (B) determine surface hardness

    (C) strengthen journal bearing surfaces

    (D) determine if the crank has been demagnetized

13. _____

14. The primary advantage of using a fluorescent penetrant
test is _____.

    (A) test results can be seen on discolored metal

    (B) test results will indicate only serious flaws

    (C) further interpretation of results is unnecessary

    (D) it can be used on both ferrous and nonferrous metals

14. _____

15. What type(s) of loads are imposed on a crankshaft
when it is in service?

    (A) Bending.

    (B) Twisting.

    (C) Both of the above.

    (D) Neither of the above.

15. _____

16. Main bearing bore misalignment, improperly
fitted bearings, loose or broken bearing caps, and
unbalanced drive pulleys can all cause what type(s)
of crankshaft failure?

    (A) Bending fatigue.

    (B) Twisting or torsional failure.

    (C) Both of the above.

    (D) Neither of the above.

16. _____

17. Abnormal engine speeds and load conditions cause
crankshaft twisting vibrations that may lead to _____.

    (A) less harmful exhaust emissions

    (B) torsional failures

    (C) static balance

    (D) None of the above.

17. _____

18. Which type of precision measuring instrument should
be used to measure crankshaft journals for taper?

    (A) Dial indicator.

    (B) Depth micrometer.

    (C) Inside micrometer.

    (D) Outside micrometer.

18. _____

19. Which type of precision measuring instrument should be used to check the alignment or straightness of a crankshaft?

    (A) Dial indicator.

    (B) Depth micrometer.

    (C) Inside micrometer.

    (D) Outside micrometer.

19. _____

20. When a crankshaft is centrifugally balanced while in motion, the process is called _____ balancing.

20. _____

21. Which of the following methods may be used to recondition the main and rod journals?

    (A) Crankshaft grinding.

    (B) Chromium plating and metal spraying.

    (C) Electro-welding.

    (D) All of the above.

21. _____

Bearing Inspection

22. The ability of a bearing material to let small particles of dirt and metal sink into it to avoid scratching the crankshaft journal is called _____.

    (A) seizure resistance

    (B) corrosion resistance

    (C) conformability

    (D) embeddability

22. _____

23. A bearing material's ability to creep or flow slightly so that the shaft and bearing will fit together better is called _____.

    (A) seizure resistance

    (B) corrosion resistance

    (C) conformability

    (D) embeddability

23. _____

Name _____

24. A bearing material's ability to withstand metal-to-metal contact without being destroyed is called _____.
    (A) seizure resistance
    (B) corrosion resistance
    (C) conformability
    (D) embeddability

24. _____

25. The ability of a bearing to resist attack by caustic chemical compounds in lubricating oil is called _____.
    (A) seizure resistance
    (B) corrosion resistance
    (C) conformability
    (D) embeddability

25. _____

26. The following metals are used in diesel engine bearing designs *except:*
    (A) steel.
    (B) magnesium.
    (C) copper-lead.
    (D) aluminum.

26. _____

27. Which type of bearing is most commonly used for connecting rod journal bearings?
    (A) Split bearings.
    (B) Full-round bearings.
    (C) Flanged thrust bearings.
    (D) Poured babbit bearings.

27. _____

28. Two designs used in engine bearings to prevent their rotation or sideways shifting in their housing are tangs or locating lugs and _____ _____.

28. _____

29. To make sure that lubricating oil holes in the crankshaft always have a passageway to provide adequate oil to all parts of the bearing surfaces, a single _____ _____ is built into most main bearings that fit into the block adjacent to the oil feed hole.

29. _____

30. Bearings with a greater wall thickness that are used to compensate for excessive journal clearance caused by excessive wear are known as _____ bearings.
    (A) oversize
    (B) undersize
    (C) standard size
    (D) eccentric

30. _____

31. Bearings that are specifically designed to increase the wedge effect needed to build the oil film under loaded areas while allowing a reduction of vertical oil clearance without reducing the effectiveness of oil flow are called _____ bearings.

    (A) oversize

    (B) undersize

    (C) standard size

    (D) eccentric

31. _____

32. Which major cause of bearing failure occurs most frequently?

    (A) Lack of lubrication.

    (B) Incorrect installation.

    (C) Overloading.

    (D) Oil-borne dirt and abrasives.

32. _____

33. Bearing problems may be detected *before* they become severe by inspecting the bearing shells and backs for grooves, pits, and corrosion during overhaul and performing a(n) _____ _____ on the used engine oil.

    (A) fatigue test

    (B) static balance

    (C) laboratory analysis

    (D) All of the above.

33. _____

34. Using _____ _____ and some arithmetic is a common method of determining oil clearance in bearings without using Plastigage.

    (A) torque specifications

    (B) micrometer measurements

    (C) locating dowels

    (D) gear ratios

34. _____

35. If Plastigage is used to check bearing clearance, which of the following operations must be performed to get an accurate measurement?

    (A) Measurements must be made in different locations on the journal's diameter.

    (B) All Plastigage must be removed before continuing assembling the engine.

    (C) Both of the above.

    (D) Neither of the above.

35. _____

Name _____

36. When an oil seal is used in an application where there
is oil on both sides of the seal, which type of seal
must be used to prevent leakage past the seal in either
direction?

   (A) Front oil seal.

   (B) Rear oil seal.

   (C) Single-lip oil seal.

   (D) Double-lip oil seal.

36. _____

37. Worn or damaged oil seals are often indicated
by _____.

   (A) elevated engine temperatures

   (B) oil leaks

   (C) noisy engine operation

   (D) excessive exhaust smoke

37. _____

38. When should crankshaft gears be removed?

   (A) Rear seal replacement.

   (B) During injection pump removal.

   (C) Whenever the timing cover is removed.

   (D) Replacement purposes only.

38. _____

39. When replacing a crankshaft gear, it is usually
necessary to _____.

   (A) heat the gear first

   (B) rebore the engine cylinders

   (C) taper the crankshaft snout with a grinding machine

   (D) use a steel hammer to drive the gear on

39. _____

40. All of the following are functions of the flywheel
except:

   (A) it provides a drive for the starting motor via a ring
gear.

   (B) it controls axial thrust of the crankshaft.

   (C) it limits the increase or decrease in speed during
sudden load changes.

   (D) it helps force the pistons through the compression
stroke when the engine is idling.

40. _____

41. Which of the following would *not* cause a flywheel to have to be resurfaced?
    (A) Damaged teeth on the ring gear.
    (B) Distortion.
    (C) Heat checks.
    (D) Scoring.

41. _____

42. When installing a starter ring gear onto a flywheel, which way should the bevel of the gear teeth be oriented?
    (A) Toward the crankshaft.
    (B) Away from the crankshaft.
    (C) Either direction.
    (D) Starter ring gears aren't beveled.

42. _____

43. Which of the following heating methods should be avoided when installing a ring gear onto a flywheel?
    (A) Heating the ring in an electric oven.
    (B) Heating the ring in a hot oil bath.
    (C) Heating the ring by direct application of a torch.
    (D) Heating the ring by using a torch to heat a plate supporting the ring gear.

43. _____

44. Which of the following vibration dampers or harmonic balancers is most easily damaged by striking or dropping them?
    (A) Composite damper.
    (B) Viscous damper.
    (C) Single-piece damper.
    (D) Two-piece damper.

44. _____

45. The _____ a crankshaft, the more difficult it is to control torsional vibrations.
    (A) lighter
    (B) heavier
    (C) shorter
    (D) longer

45. _____

Name _____

Date_____

Instructor_____

Score_____ Text pages 131–152

Chapter 7

Pistons, Rings, and Connecting Rods

After studying this chapter and completing supplemental exercises, you will be able to:

- Explain the functions of the piston.
- Name the key parts of a piston and detail what they do.
- Describe piston service.
- Explain the functions of piston rings.
- Describe how to install piston rings.
- Explain the function of the connecting rod.
- Describe how to install a piston assembly into a cylinder block.

Diesel Pistons

1. All of the following are primary components of the piston assembly *except* the:

(A) oil ring.

(B) connecting rod.

(C) main bearing.

(D) compression ring.

1. _____

2. Pistons fit inside what part of the engine block?

    (A) Intake manifold.

    (B) Lower crankcase.

    (C) Cylinders.

    (D) Exhaust manifold.

2. _____

3. Pistons perform all of the following functions *except:*

    (A) receiving and transmitting combustion forces to the crankshaft.

    (B) absorbing and dissipating heat from the combustion chamber.

    (C) controlling the opening and shutting of the exhaust valves.

    (D) supporting the side thrust of the connecting rod.

3. _____

4. The top section of the piston is known as the _____.

    (A) skirt

    (B) crown

    (C) groove

    (D) land

4. _____

5. The top section of the piston often has reliefs cast or machined into it to provide clearance for what components when the piston is at top dead center?

    (A) Valves.

    (B) Rings.

    (C) Pin.

    (D) Boss.

5. _____

6. The combustion cup is located on what part of a diesel engine piston?

    (A) Crown.

    (B) Skirt.

    (C) Pin bore.

    (D) Pin boss.

6. _____

7. Grooves are cut into the sides of the pistons to house which of the following components?

    (A) Rings.

    (B) Bearings.

    (C) Rods.

    (D) Skirts.

7. _____

Name _____

8. Piston lands are the areas between the piston grooves
   and are smaller at the _____ of the piston.
   (A) side
   (B) base
   (C) top
   (D) bottom

8. _____

9. Which area of the piston is closer to the heat source?
   (A) Head.
   (B) Skirt.
   (C) Pin.
   (D) Cooling nozzle.

9. _____

10. The piston area that extends from the lowest ring
    groove to the bottom of the piston is called the _____.
    (A) crown
    (B) boss
    (C) web
    (D) skirt

10. _____

11. The modern version of the trunk piston, the _____
    _____ _____ is designed to better handle higher
    cylinder pressures and temperatures on today's
    diesel engines.

11. _____

12. A two-piece piston designed to reduce side-loading on
    the piston skirt area is a(n) _____ piston.

12. _____

13. On a two-piece piston design, if the skirt is damaged, it
    can be reconditioned using a specialized _____ process.

13. _____

14. Cam ground pistons are slightly elliptical rather than
    perfectly round to compensate for _____.
    (A) unequal compression pressures
    (B) out-of-round piston rings
    (C) uneven heat expansion during operation
    (D) elliptical cylinder bores

14. _____

15. When are cam ground pistons as close to being
    perfectly round as they will get?
    (A) At the end of their useful service life.
    (B) Before being installed into the engine.
    (C) When the engine is first cranked cold.
    (D) When the engine has reached operating
        temperature.

15. _____

16. Which of the following methods safely and effectively removes buildup and prevents damage to piston surfaces?

    (A) Using solvent or detergent solution.

    (B) Scraping the piston with a groove cleaner.

    (C) Soaking in gasoline.

    (D) Using a smooth grinding wheel on a bench grinder.

16. _____

17. During piston inspection, which of the following would most likely indicate a lack of oil spray on the underside of the piston?

    (A) Burned spots or carbon formation.

    (B) Worn lands.

    (C) Excessive ring wear.

    (D) Cracked piston.

17. _____

18. Which of the following would be an acceptable method of repairing and reusing a cracked piston?

    (A) Resurfacing the piston.

    (B) Pinning the crack.

    (C) Relieving the cracked area in a lathe.

    (D) None of the above.

18. _____

19. Piston clearance between the piston and the cylinder wall is necessary to _____.

    (A) make certain that the rings fit tightly in the cylinder

    (B) ensure there is enough room for thermal expansion of the piston

    (C) prevent the piston pin from contacting the cylinder wall

    (D) prevent oil from reaching the compression ring

19. _____

Piston Rings

20. Which of the following is *not* a function of the piston rings?

    (A) To prevent oil from reaching the piston pin area.

    (B) To form a tight seal between the piston and cylinder.

    (C) To transfer heat in order to cool the piston.

    (D) To help maintain proper lubrication between the piston and the cylinder wall.

20. _____

Name _____

21. Compression rings are designed to _____.
    (A) prevent gases from leaking by the piston
    (B) increase blowby
    (C) force oil on the cylinder walls into the combustion area
    (D) push exhaust gases into the intake manifold

21. _____

22. Intermediate rings control about _____ % of the compression and combustion pressures.
    (A) 50
    (B) 25
    (C) 10
    (D) 0

22. _____

23. All of the following intermediate ring designs are commonly found in diesel engine applications *except:*
    (A) butt joint.
    (B) angled joint.
    (C) lap joint.
    (D) solid joint.

23. _____

24. Oil control rings are typically located in which grooves of the piston?
    (A) Upper.
    (B) Middle.
    (C) Lower.
    (D) Intermediate.

24. _____

25. To check for piston groove wear, _____.
    (A) measure ring protrusion from the surface of adjacent lands
    (B) measure side clearance between old ring and the upper land of the groove
    (C) measure side clearance between a new ring and the upper land of the groove
    (D) measure distance between upper and lower land with ring removed

25. _____

26. When installing piston rings, the ring gaps must be _____.
    (A) aligned so all gaps are in a row
    (B) staggered so none of the gaps are in a row
    (C) totally closed up to control compression and combustion pressures
    (D) None of the above.

26. _____

Piston Pins (Wrist Pins)

27. All of the following methods are used in piston pin designs *except:*
    (A) fixed pin.
    (B) variable pin.
    (C) semi-floating pin.
    (D) full-floating pin.

27. _____

28. The reinforced area around the piston pin hole is called the pin _____.
    (A) escutcheon
    (B) web
    (C) float
    (D) boss

28. _____

29. Based on their design, _____ _____ should be checked for clearance in both the piston and connecting rod.
    (A) ring expanders
    (B) full-floating pins
    (C) fixed pins
    (D) None of the above.

29. _____

Connecting Rods

30. The connecting rod _____.
    (A) connects the crankshaft to the camshaft
    (B) connects the rings to the piston
    (C) connects the piston to the crankshaft
    (D) connects the cylinder to the piston

30. _____

31. A fracture split connecting rod features a(n) _____ and _____ that are divided using a rough impact breakage process instead of being evenly machine cut.
    (A) piston skirt, crown
    (B) piston pin, bushing
    (C) cap, yoke
    (D) All of the above.

31. _____

Name _____

32. Which of the following should be checked when inspecting rods?

    (A) Magnetic particle checks for cracks.

    (B) Out-of-roundness of crank bore.

    (C) Twist and bend.

    (D) All of the above.

32. _____

33. When should a cracked connecting rod be reused?

    (A) After rewelding.

    (B) After re-machining.

    (C) After heating to relax stress-risers in the crack area.

    (D) Never.

33. _____

34. When installing the main bearings, care should be taken to do all of the following *except*:

    (A) thoroughly clean each bore and the back of each bearing.

    (B) rub the bearings with a coarse-grade abrasive.

    (C) make sure the locating lugs fit into the notches provided.

    (D) install upper front and rear thrust washers at proper main bearing locations.

34. _____

35. Excessive lubrication of main bearing bolt threads can cause hydraulic lock when the bolts are _____ to their specified settings.

    (A) cut

    (B) hand-tightened

    (C) torqued

    (D) balanced

35. _____

36. When checking main bearing clearance with Plastigage on an engine in an upright position, _____ weight must be removed from the lower half of the bearing being checked.

    (A) crankshaft

    (B) cylinder head

    (C) connecting rod

    (D) All of the above.

36. _____

37. If binding occurs when installing the piston into the block, the technician should _____.

    (A) use a press to force the piston into the liner

    (B) use more lubricant

    (C) tighten the ring compressor before continuing

    (D) remove the piston and make necessary corrections

37. _____

38. When installing pistons, the corresponding rod throw should be positioned _____.

    (A) at top dead center

    (B) at bottom dead center

    (C) 90° after top dead center

    (D) 90° after bottom dead center

38. _____

39. After installing the pistons, the connecting rod side clearance should be checked with a(n) _____.

    (A) multimeter

    (B) ring compressor

    (C) torque wrench

    (D) feeler or dial indicator

39. _____

40. Oil seals should be replaced only _____.

    (A) if the seal surface on the crankshaft is grooved

    (B) if the seal has been leaking

    (C) if the crankshaft has been reground

    (D) in pairs, anytime major overhauls are performed

40. _____

Name _____

Date _____

Instructor _____

Score _____ Text pages 153–178

Chapter 8

Cylinder Heads and Related Components

After studying this chapter and completing supplemental exercises, you will be able to:

• List the parts that are attached to the cylinder head.
• Explain cylinder head disassembly procedures.
• Explain how to check for cracks and leaks in a cylinder head.
• Name five problems common to cylinder heads.
• Describe the service of valves and related components.

Cylinder Head

1. Name the two materials that generally make up cylinder heads.

_____

_____

2. The cylinder head houses all of the following components *except:*

(A) the piston.

(B) valves.

(C) fuel injectors.

(D) valve seats.

2. _____

3. Cylinder head studs are generally _____.

    (A) threaded on only one end

    (B) threaded on both ends

    (C) threaded along their entire length

    (D) pressed into the block and have no threads

3. _____

4. When torquing cylinder head studs, the nuts should be torqued _____.

    (A) from the outer edge, working toward the center of the head

    (B) from the center of the head, working to the outside

    (C) from the rear of the head, working toward the front

    (D) from the front of the head, working toward the rear

4. _____

5. The following tools are accepted methods of removing broken studs from a block *except* for a(n):

    (A) stud extractor.

    (B) cutting torch.

    (C) locking pliers.

    (D) screw extractor.

5. _____

6. Combustion gases, oil, and coolant can leak from the irregularities between the block and head mating surfaces unless sealed with _____.

    (A) stuffing-box packing

    (B) RTV (room temperature vulcanization) compound

    (C) special sealing wax

    (D) a compressible gasket

6. _____

7. The only way to verify _____ _____ of a cylinder head gasket is for a technician to remove the cylinder head and inspect the internal passages and chambers.

    (A) torque specifications

    (B) broken studs

    (C) internal leakage

    (D) heat ratings

7. _____

8. When should a head gasket be reused?

    (A) When there is no visible damage to the gasket.

    (B) When a new or resurfaced head is being installed.

    (C) Only when visible damage has been repaired.

    (D) Never.

8. _____

Name _____

9. To start cylinder head disassembly, what are the first components that should be removed?

   (A) Intake and exhaust manifolds.

   (B) Valve covers.

   (C) Rocker arms.

   (D) Crankcase vent breather element.

9. _____

10. If rocker arm assemblies are to be reused, the technician should be sure to _____.

   (A) replace pushrod cups

   (B) resurface valve tips where they contact the rocker arm

   (C) reinstall the rocker arms in the exact position from which they were removed

   (D) avoid reinstalling the rocker arms in the position from which they were removed

10. _____

11. When removing a cylinder head from the engine, it is good practice to protect the injector nozzles from damage by _____.

   (A) removing the nozzles before removing the head

   (B) loosening the nozzle clamps

   (C) turning the head upside down so the nozzles will not contact the worktable surface

   (D) leaving the nozzles torqued in the head to prevent distortion

11. _____

12. To prevent contamination of the fuel injectors, _____.

   (A) do not remove the fuel lines from the nozzles

   (B) blow out the fuel lines and fittings with compressed air

   (C) immerse the injectors and fittings in clean diesel fuel while disconnected

   (D) plug or cap off the lines and fittings

12. _____

13. To prevent cylinder head distortion during removal, _____.

   (A) remove the head after it has cooled to room temperature

   (B) remove the head while it is still hot

   (C) remove the bolts and dislodge the head by prying from the exhaust manifold side

   (D) remove the bolts and use a large steel hammer to dislodge the head

13. _____

14. To remove the valves from the head, _____.   14. _____

   (A) use a torch to remove the valve spring retainers

   (B) use a hammer and a deep-well socket to dislodge the valve spring retainers

   (C) use a soft hammer to strike the edge of the spring to dislodge the keepers

   (D) use a valve spring compressor to compress the springs

15. What type of personal protection should be used when removing valves from a head?   15. _____

   (A) Face and eye protection.

   (B) Gloves to prevent burns.

   (C) Work apron to prevent oil from saturating the technicians work clothes.

   (D) Earplugs to protect hearing from hammer blows.

16. Cylinder heads should be cleaned _____.   16. _____

   (A) only after magnetic particle inspection is complete

   (B) only after fluorescent penetrant testing is complete

   (C) before they are inspected

   (D) before they are removed from the engine

17. The following are all commonly used methods to check cylinder heads for cracks *except*:   17. _____

   (A) fluorescent penetrant.

   (B) deglazing.

   (C) pressure.

   (D) spot-check dye.

18. The method of checking a head for cracks by sealing the openings with plates or plugs and immersing it in water is called the _____ method.   18. _____

   (A) pressure

   (B) spot-check dye

   (C) magnaflux

   (D) fluorescent penetrant

19. The best method of checking heads for cracks in areas that cannot be seen is the _____ method.   19. _____

   (A) pressure

   (B) spot-check dye

   (C) magnaflux

   (D) fluorescent penetrant

Name _____

20. Which of the following methods can be used only on ferrous (cast iron) heads?

    (A) Pressure.

    (B) Spot-check dye.

    (C) Magnaflux.

    (D) Fluorescent penetrant.

20. _____

21. Cylinder head warpage can be caused by all of the following conditions *except:*

    (A) removing the head while it is hot.

    (B) removing the head while it is cold.

    (C) improper tightening of cylinder head bolts.

    (D) improper casting or machining procedures.

21. _____

22. All of the following are symptoms of fouling *except:*

    (A) high compression.

    (B) overheating.

    (C) smoky exhaust.

    (D) low power.

22. _____

23. Burning and corrosion of the cylinder head and the block mating surface is usually caused by _____.

    (A) a defective gasket

    (B) using the wrong grade diesel fuel

    (C) long periods of idling

    (D) extended oil change intervals

23. _____

24. The rate of corrosion may often be accelerated by _____.

    (A) using full synthetic engine oil

    (B) worn bearings

    (C) using the wrong gasket

    (D) improper coolant treatment

24. _____

Valves

25. The valves generally used in internal combustion engines are called_____ valves.

    (A) compensating

    (B) Schrader

    (C) ball cock

    (D) poppet

25. _____

26. The tapered area machined at an angle on the valve head is called the _____.
    (A) stem
    (B) seat
    (C) face
    (D) margin

26. _____

27. The part of the valve that provides a place to connect the valve spring to the valve is the _____.
    (A) stem
    (B) seat
    (C) face
    (D) margin

27. _____

28. The area between the valve face and the valve head is called the _____.
    (A) stem
    (B) seat
    (C) guide
    (D) margin

28. _____

29. Which valves typically use high-alloy steel and hard alloys such as Stellite to increase their wear qualities and heat resistance?
    (A) Intake valves.
    (B) Exhaust valves.
    (C) Both of the above.
    (D) Neither of the above.

29. _____

30. Which surface(s) of a valve can be resurfaced?
    (A) Valve face.
    (B) Valve tip.
    (C) Both of the above.
    (D) Neither of the above.

30. _____

31. As a general rule, it is not advisable to grind a valve face to the point where the margin is reduced by more than _____.
    (A) 5%
    (B) 25%
    (C) 50%
    (D) Margin may never be reduced.

31. _____

Name _____

32. To eliminate stem flexing from the pressure of the
    grinding wheel, valves should be chucked as close to
    the _____ as possible.
    (A) tip
    (B) head
    (C) stem
    (D) collet groove

32. _____

33. Valve guide clearance should be very small to facilitate
    all of the following *except:*
    (A) causing oil to be drawn into the combustion chamber.
    (B) keeping the valve cool.
    (C) preventing combustion gases from entering the
        crankcase.
    (D) keeping the valve face in perfect alignment with
        the valve seat.

33. _____

34. In guide repair, the method that provides better
    lubrication, excellent wear qualities, and tight
    clearances (but is the most expensive and difficult to
    install) is _____.
    (A) knurling
    (B) reaming
    (C) thin-wall inserts
    (D) threaded bronze inserts

34. _____

35. Increasing the diameter of the valve guide hole so that
    it may be fitted with an oversize valve stem is known
    as _____.
    (A) knurling
    (B) reaming
    (C) thin-wall inserts
    (D) threaded bronze inserts

35. _____

36. As a rule of thumb, _____ guides should be driven out
    toward the combustion chamber.
    (A) stepped
    (B) flanged
    (C) integral
    (D) straight

36. _____

37. Because of the close interference fit, insert guides should be _____ before being pressed into the head.
    (A) threaded
    (B) heated
    (C) chilled
    (D) knurled

37. _____

38. Valve seats are precision ground to form a tight seal with the valve _____.
    (A) face
    (B) stem
    (C) guide
    (D) tip

38. _____

39. Leakage between the valve face and the valve seat usually leads to _____.
    (A) reduced engine compression
    (B) reduced engine power
    (C) Both of the above.
    (D) Neither of the above.

39. _____

40. The area of the valve face between the contact area and the valve margin is known as _____.
    (A) expansion
    (B) precision
    (C) overhang
    (D) concentricity

40. _____

41. Valve seats that are added to the cylinder head after casting are known as what type of seat?
    (A) Integral seats.
    (B) Insert seats.
    (C) Precision seats.
    (D) Supplemental seats.

41. _____

42. Seats that are an actual part of the original head casting are known as _____ seats.
    (A) integral
    (B) insert
    (C) precision
    (D) supplemental

42. _____

Name _____

43. A properly ground seat has how many angles?   43. _____
    (A) One.
    (B) Two.
    (C) Three.
    (D) Four.

44. The variance formed when the valve face and the   44. _____
    valve seat are machined at slightly different angles is
    referred to as an _____.
    (A) interrupted angle
    (B) induced angle
    (C) intrepid angle
    (D) interference angle

45. While checking an insert seat for tightness, a   45. _____
    technician positions a drift on top of the insert and
    lightly taps the end of the drift with a hammer. A
    ringing sound is heard, indicating that the seat is _____.
    (A) loose
    (B) tight
    (C) out-of-round
    (D) recessed too far into the relief

46. When replacing an insert valve seat, the depth of the 46. _____
    counterbore must be determined to properly install
    the new seat. The proper measuring instrument for
    determining this measurement is a_____.
    (A) concentricity gauge
    (B) drift punch
    (C) depth micrometer
    (D) dial indicator

47. When using Prussian blue to determine the concentricity 47. _____
    of a valve seat insert relative to the valve guide, a
    properly ground valve seat should have Prussian blue
    visible around _____ of the insert diameter.
    (A) all
    (B) only half
    (C) only a quarter
    (D) none

48. Which of the following does *not* fall into the general category of valve seals?
    (A) Deflector seals.
    (B) Permanent seals.
    (C) Positive seals.
    (D) O-ring seals.

48. _____

49. One of the most common types of seal is the umbrella seal. Which general category does this type of seal fall into?
    (A) Deflector seals.
    (B) Permanent seals.
    (C) Positive seals.
    (D) O-ring seals.

49. _____

50. Valve stem seals are generally made of _____.
    (A) acrylic compounds
    (B) ceramic composite
    (C) sintered brass
    (D) synthetic rubber

50. _____

51. When installing a new valve stem seal, using a design of seal *not* specified by the engine manufacturer may cause _____.
    (A) seal failure
    (B) reduced emissions
    (C) cylinder head warpage
    (D) improved engine thermal efficiency

51. _____

52. What type of valve springs are used by most manufacturers?
    (A) Compound.
    (B) Reverse wound.
    (C) Leaf.
    (D) Cylindrical.

52. _____

53. To reduce vibration and assist in reducing valve spring surge at high speeds, many valve spring arrangements use a smaller inner spring referred to as a _____.
    (A) progressive coil
    (B) damper coil
    (C) compound coil
    (D) mortal coil

53. _____

Name _____

54. The valve spring itself is held in place by the valve spring retainer, which is locked onto the valve stem with two wedge-shaped parts called valve keepers or _____.

    (A) deflectors

    (B) collets

    (C) rings

    (D) chucks

54. _____

55. The type of valve spring pressure that overcomes valve train inertia is _____ pressure.

    (A) open

    (B) close

    (C) reverse

    (D) compound

55. _____

56. When using a dial spring pressure tester to check valve spring pressures, all pressures should be within _____ of the service manual's specifications.

    (A) 1%

    (B) 10%

    (C) 25%

    (D) 50%

56. _____

57. When checking release-type rotators for proper clearance, clearance should be checked between the valve tip and the valve tip _____.

    (A) bowl

    (B) cup

    (C) plate

    (D) retainer

57. _____

58. What type of maintenance is required for positive-type rotators?

    (A) Weekly.

    (B) Monthly.

    (C) Yearly.

    (D) None.

58. _____

59. Valve keepers (locks) fit into keeper grooves that are
    machined into the end of the valve _____.
    (A) retainer
    (B) spring
    (C) seal
    (D) stem

59. _____

60. Fuel injection nozzle bores are usually machined into
    the _____.
    (A) injector body
    (B) cylinder head
    (C) cylinder block
    (D) intake manifold

60. _____

Name _____

Date_____

Instructor_____

Score_____ Text pages 179–200

Chapter 9

Camshaft and Valve Train Components

After studying this chapter and completing supplemental exercises, you will be able to:

- Remove and replace a diesel engine camshaft.
- Explain the operation of the valve train components.
- Determine the causes of valve guide wear.
- Describe the operation of a gear train.
- Identify and explain the purpose of various components of the valve timing drive assembly.
- Explain how to assemble valve train components.

Valve Train Operating Mechanisms

1. The group of components that collectively function to open and close a diesel engine's intake and exhaust valves is referred to as the _____.

    (A) valve ensemble

    (B) valve train

    (C) valve composite

    (D) valve gearing

1. _____

2. Acting as a mechanical computer, what component synchronizes the operation of the valves and fuel injectors with the action of the pistons?

(A) Counter shaft.

(B) Idler shaft.

(C) Crankshaft.

(D) Camshaft.

2. _____

3. The signals for opening and closing the valves and for triggering the injectors are determined by the _____ design.

(A) cam lobe

(B) lifter

(C) distributor

(D) rocker arm

3. _____

4. Instead of being round, like the rest of the camshaft, cam lobes have what type of shape?

(A) Triangular.

(B) Parabolic.

(C) Eccentric.

(D) Concentric.

4. _____

5. In most modern mobile diesels, the cam lobes are a(n) _____ part of the camshaft.

(A) detachable

(B) replaceable

(C) adjustable

(D) integral

5. _____

6. To reduce wear, camshafts are made of _____.

(A) low-carbon alloy steel

(B) aluminum

(C) ferro-chromium alloy

(D) machined magnesium billets

6. _____

7. The camshaft gear is twice as large as the crankshaft gear in a(n) _____ engine.

(A) reciprocating

(B) naturally aspirated

(C) two-stroke cycle

(D) four-stroke cycle

7. _____

Name _____

8. The camshaft gear is the same size as the crankshaft   8. _____
   gear in a(n) _____ engine.
   (A) reciprocating
   (B) naturally aspirated
   (C) two-stroke cycle
   (D) four-stroke cycle

9. The maximum lift occurs at the _____ of the cam lobe.   9. _____
   (A) apex
   (B) duplex
   (C) base circle
   (D) heel

10. In most mobile diesel engines, the camshaft drive gear   10. _____
    is keyed and pressed onto the camshaft while riding
    on a(n) _____ _____, which is retained by two bolts.

11. When rocker arms are used to open the valves, the   11. _____
    difference between cam lift and valve lift is known as
    the _____.
    (A) cam lobe ratio
    (B) valve lift ratio
    (C) cam angle ratio
    (D) rocker arm ratio

12. The _____ of the cam lobe determines the amount of   12. _____
    time the valve is open.
    (A) duration angle
    (B) proportional lift
    (C) base circle tangent
    (D) centerline angle

13. The camshaft may be located in the _____ _____ or   13. _____
    the _____ _____.

    _____

14. Engines with camshafts located in the cylinder block _____.
    (A) don't exist
    (B) are referred to as overhead valve engines
    (C) are referred to as overhead cam engines
    (D) are referred to as integral oriented engines

14. _____

15. Engines with camshafts located in the cylinder head _____.
    (A) don't exist
    (B) are referred to as overhead valve engines
    (C) are referred to as overhead cam engines
    (D) are referred to as integral oriented engines

15. _____

16. Which type of engine always uses push rods?
    (A) Air-cooled engines.
    (B) Overhead valve engines.
    (C) Overhead cam engines.
    (D) Integral oriented engines.

16. _____

17. A condition where the valve is momentarily thrown free from the direct influence of the cam lobe is referred to as _____.
    (A) valve drift
    (B) valve flux
    (C) valve float
    (D) valve inertia

17. _____

18. The group of components that takes power from the crankshaft and transfers it to the camshaft is known as the _____.
    (A) camshaft drive system
    (B) redux reciprocal system
    (C) drive ratio system
    (D) power derivative system

18. _____

19. Which type of drive can be used to transfer motion from the crankshaft to the camshaft?
    (A) Gear drive.
    (B) Chain drive.
    (C) Belt drive.
    (D) All of the above.

19. _____

Name _____

20. When the drive mechanism consists only of gears, it is commonly referred to as a(n) _____.

    (A) cogged system

    (B) power derivative system

    (C) gear train

    (D) power train

20. _____

21. Accessory drives on diesel engines may be located _____.

    (A) in the front of the engine

    (B) in the rear of the engine

    (C) Either of the above.

    (D) Neither of the above.

21. _____

22. When two mating gears have a different number of teeth, the number of times the driving gear turns for each revolution of the driven gear is known as gear _____.

    (A) interface

    (B) meshment

    (C) profile

    (D) ratio

22. _____

23. In most industrial applications of chain drive systems, both the crankshaft gear and the camshaft gear are made of _____.

    (A) steel

    (B) brass

    (C) nylon

    (D) aluminum

23. _____

24. Maintaining the relationship between camshaft and crankshaft to properly control the opening and closing of the valves is called _____.

    (A) synchronicity

    (B) engine timing

    (C) valve overlap

    (D) valve lash

24. _____

25. How fast a valve opens and closes is determined by
    the _____ of the cam lobe.
    (A) ratio
    (B) material makeup
    (C) duration
    (D) slope

25. _____

26. What are the advantages of using a variable valve timing system in a diesel engine?

    _____

    _____

    _____

    _____

27. The cam lobe's eccentric shape is translated into
    reciprocating motion and transferred either to the push
    rod or directly to the rocker arm by the _____.
    (A) rocker arm pivot
    (B) cam bearing
    (C) gear ratio
    (D) lifter cam follower

27. _____

28. Valve lifters in most inline diesel engines are of what type?
    (A) Hydraulic.
    (B) Pneumatic.
    (C) Desmodramic.
    (D) Solid.

28. _____

29. Clearance between parts of the valve train is necessary
    to _____.
    (A) allow for mechanical failures
    (B) allow for cooling
    (C) allow for thermal expansion
    (D) allow for normal component wear

29. _____

30. When the follower rides directly on the camshaft lobe
    and transmits cam motion directly to the valve and
    injector, it is called a(n) _____ _____ follower.

30. _____

Name _____

31. When two valves are opened simultaneously by a single rocker arm, the mechanism that bridges the two valves together is called a(n) _____.

    (A) crosshead

    (B) duo-push

    (C) bridge cap

    (D) divider

31. _____

32. Valves and followers are generally lubricated by _____.

    (A) high pressure nozzles

    (B) high temperature grease

    (C) overflow oil from the rocker arms

    (D) manual operations

32. _____

33. Rocker housing covers are usually sealed with a gasket and designed to _____.

    (A) equalize pressure between the combustion chamber and the crankcase

    (B) provide a mounting surface for the rocker arms

    (C) keep dirt out of the engine

    (D) facilitate cooling by convection

33. _____

Inspecting and Servicing the Valve Train

34. When checking the cam bearing ID in an engine block, a technician discovers that the ID exceeds the tolerance given in the service manual. Additionally, the bearings are scratched and scored. The technician should _____.

    (A) replace the cam

    (B) replace the block

    (C) replace the bearings

    (D) machine the block for oversized bearings

34. _____

35. The simplest way to measure camshaft lobes for wear is to use a(n) _____.

    (A) a depth micrometer

    (B) an inside caliper

    (C) a go/no-go gauge

    (D) an outside micrometer

35. _____

36. Camshaft straightness or runout should be checked with a(n) _____.
    (A) a dial indicator
    (B) an inside caliper
    (C) a go/no-go gauge
    (D) an outside micrometer

36. _____

37. Lifter bores should be measured with a(n) _____.
    (A) depth micrometer
    (B) inside caliper
    (C) dial bore gauge
    (D) outside micrometer

37. _____

38. The repair procedure for worn rocker arm bushings is the same as that for _____.
    (A) grinding valves
    (B) ring grooves
    (C) concave lifters
    (D) piston pin bushings

38. _____

39. Push rods should be checked for all of the following *except:*
    (A) hardness.
    (B) bends.
    (C) cracks.
    (D) worn tips.

39. _____

Assembling the Valve Train Components

40. In what order should camshaft bearings be installed back into a block?
    (A) Front to back.
    (B) Back to front.
    (C) Each end, working toward the center.
    (D) From the center, working toward each end.

40. _____

Name _____

41. If the camshaft journals were reground, the
    replacement cam bearings will have to be _____ than
    the original bearings.

    (A) wider

    (B) narrower

    (C) thicker

    (D) thinner

41. _____

42. Once installed, the camshaft should be checked for
    _____.

    (A) binding

    (B) end play

    (C) runout

    (D) All of the above.

42. _____

43. Before assembling the serviced valve train operating
    mechanisms, which of the following measurements is
    deemed critical?

    (A) Installed valve stem height.

    (B) Installed valve spring height.

    (C) Both of the above.

    (D) Neither of the above.

43. _____

44. When checking total indicated runout (TIR) of installed
    camshaft gears, the measurements on the dial indicator
    should be computed as follows:

    (A) Regard only the maximum reading on the plus side
        of zero.

    (B) Regard only the maximum reading on the minus
        side of zero.

    (C) Subtract the maximum minus reading from the
        maximum plus reading.

    (D) Add the maximum minus reading to the maximum
        plus reading.

44. _____

45. The amount of "play" between two gears in mesh is
    referred to as _____.

    (A) end play

    (B) backlash

    (C) total indicated runout (TIR)

    (D) None of the above.

45. _____

46. Which precision instrument can be used to check the head depth of valves before the cylinder head is attached to the engine?

    (A) Dial indicator.

    (B) Depth micrometer.

    (C) Either of the above.

    (D) Neither of the above.

46. _____

47. When torquing cylinder head studs, the nuts should be torqued _____.

    (A) from the outer edge, working toward the center of the head

    (B) from the center of the head, working to the outside

    (C) from the rear of the head, working toward the front

    (D) from the front of the head, working toward the rear

47. _____

48. When the valves are properly adjusted, the small clearance between the valve stem and the end of the rocker arm is generally referred to as valve _____.

    (A) flux

    (B) slop

    (C) lash

    (D) gap

48. _____

49. Typical valve adjustment for an OHV engine begins by positioning the number one piston at _____.

    (A) top dead center

    (B) bottom dead center

    (C) 90° before top dead center

    (D) 90° before bottom dead center

49. _____

Name _____

Date_____

Instructor_____

Score_____ Text pages 201–230

Chapter 10

Lubrication Systems

After studying this chapter and completing supplemental exercises, you will be able to:

- Explain how oil flows through the lubrication system.
- Name the four primary tasks of lubricating oil.
- Describe the two types of lubrication systems employed in diesel engines.
- Explain the operation of the various types of oil pumps used in diesel engines.
- Explain the purpose of an oil cooler.
- Name the different classifications of oil filters and explain how they operate.
- Describe how different types of oil filtration systems function.
- Explain the operation of various oil pressure indication systems.
- Explain the purpose of oil additives.

Lubrication Systems

1. Name the four primary jobs that engine oils perform.

_____

_____

_____

_____

Lubrication System Components

2. During normal operation, the bulk of the oil capacity is stored in the oil _____.
   (A) galleries
   (B) filter
   (C) cooler
   (D) pan or sump

2. _____

3. What component is the engine oil drawn through by the oil pump so that the oil may be delivered under pressure to the rest of the engine?
   (A) Turbo supply line.
   (B) Oil filter.
   (C) Suction pickup tube.
   (D) Main bearing journals.

3. _____

4. If too much oil is pumped into the system by the oil pump, excess oil will be returned to the inlet oil passage by the oil _____.
   (A) filter bypass valve
   (B) pressure regulator valve
   (C) dipstick
   (D) turbo supply line

4. _____

5. An engine's oil level can be checked by the use of a calibrated _____.
   (A) dipstick
   (B) pressure gauge
   (C) manometer
   (D) valve

5. _____

6. It is best to check the oil level when the engine is _____.
   (A) hot
   (B) cold
   (C) running
   (D) first started

6. _____

7. Name two types of lubrication systems.

   _____

   _____

Name _____

8. On a(n) _____ _____ lubrication system, scoops are located on the bottom of the rod caps to pick up oil and sling it onto moving parts nearby.

8. _____

9. The area of the engine that houses the crankshaft and provides a mounting surface for the oil pan is called the _____.
   (A) fire deck
   (B) flywheel housing
   (C) rocker box
   (D) crankcase

9. _____

10. The lower part of the oil pan is called the _____.
    (A) basin
    (B) sump
    (C) screen
    (D) pickup

10. _____

11. Foreign particles in the oil that could damage the engine are removed before the oil reaches the oil pump by a(n) _____.
    (A) basin
    (B) sump
    (C) pickup
    (D) screen

11. _____

12. Mobile engine pans are generally made of which of the following materials?
    (A) Steel.
    (B) Aluminum.
    (C) Plastic.
    (D) Any of the above.

12. _____

13. What enables the used engine oil to be removed from the oil pan during routine servicing?
    (A) Oil filler cap.
    (B) Oil filter petcock.
    (C) Oil pan drain plug.
    (D) Oil pan pickup tube.

13. _____

14. Before installing an oil pan gasket, the flanges of the oil pan should be checked for _____.
   (A) warpage
   (B) stripped threads
   (C) scratched protective coating
   (D) correct orientation

14. _____

15. A calibrated dipstick is used to check the oil level in the crankcase. This dipstick is generally located _____.
   (A) in the rocker cover
   (B) in the flywheel housing
   (C) in the oil pump
   (D) in the side of the cylinder block or oil pan

15. _____

16. When a boat is at rest, the oil level in a properly filled crankcase should not cover the _____.
   (A) drain plug
   (B) sea cock
   (C) rear oil seal
   (D) pickup tube

16. _____

17. Although some industrial engines may be higher, the required oil pressure for most diesel engines ranges from _____.
   (A) 3–5 psi
   (B) 25–40 psi
   (C) 300–500 psi
   (D) 250–5000 psi

17. _____

18. Oil pumps used in mobile diesel engines have a(n) _____ design.
   (A) variable displacement
   (B) negative displacement
   (C) positive displacement
   (D) diaphragm

18. _____

19. Too much internal clearance in a positive displacement oil pump will result in reduced efficiency because of internal _____.
   (A) cavitation
   (B) oil starvation
   (C) friction
   (D) leakage

19. _____

Name _____

20. Of all positive displacement pump types, which is the most commonly used in mobile diesel applications?

    (A) Internal gear pumps.

    (B) External gear pumps.

    (C) Herringbone gear pump.

    (D) Diaphragm oil pump.

20. _____

21. The external gear pump is usually driven by the _____.

    (A) idler shaft

    (B) camshaft

    (C) crankshaft

    (D) driveshaft

21. _____

22. The most common internal gear pump uses a four-lobe inner rotor and a five-lobe outer rotor and is referred to as a(n) _____ design.

    (A) crescent pump

    (B) gerotor pump

    (C) trochoidal pump

    (D) vane type pump

22. _____

23. The sliding vane type pump is usually only found in _____ mobile equipment diesels.

    (A) smaller

    (B) larger

    (C) reverse rotation

    (D) rotary

23. _____

24. To inspect and service an external gear pump, it is usually necessary to _____.

    (A) torque the mounting bolts

    (B) remove the pump from the engine

    (C) magnaflux the internal gears

    (D) have specialty tools designed specifically for this job

24. _____

25. If after disassembling an oil pump the housing is found to be damaged, it must be _____.

    (A) rebored

    (B) readjusted

    (C) realigned

    (D) replaced

25. _____

26. The greatest amount of wear in an external gear pump   26. _____
    is usually found in the _____.
    (A) housing
    (B) idler and driven gears
    (C) rotating shaft
    (D) relief valve

27. When inspecting the internal gears of an oil pump,   27. _____
    they can be checked for free play by _____ the gears.
    (A) spinning
    (B) x-raying
    (C) magnafluxing
    (D) dye-penetrant testing

28. With the gears mounted in the housing, end clearance   28. _____
    can be checked by placing a straightedge across the
    face of the gear and using a(n) _____ to measure the
    clearance.
    (A) depth gauge
    (B) feeler gauge
    (C) outside micrometer
    (D) dial indicator

29. After reassembling and installing the oil pump in the   29. _____
    gear train system, the oil pump driving gear should be
    checked for proper _____.
    (A) hardness
    (B) coloration
    (C) directional rotation
    (D) backlash

30. In the rotor-type pump, wear will occur between   30. _____
    _____.
    (A) the lobes on the inner and outer rotors
    (B) the idler gear and the housing
    (C) the drive gear and the housing
    (D) the input shaft and the inner rotor

31. Most oil pumps have a(n) _____ at the inlet to prevent   31. _____
    foreign material from entering the pump.
    (A) baffle
    (B) filter
    (C) bypass valve
    (D) screen

Name _____

32. It is necessary to cool engine oil during normal
    operations because excessive heat causes the oil
    to _____.
    (A) coagulate
    (B) increase in viscosity
    (C) oxidize and form carbon deposits
    (D) become acidic

32. _____

33. What two types of oil coolers are typically used in mobile diesel engines?

    _____

    _____

34. Tube oil coolers are usually mounted _____ on the
    side of the engine block.
    (A) internally
    (B) externally
    (C) vertically
    (D) horizontally

34. _____

35. In a typical tube oil cooler, which of the following
    flows through the cooler?
    (A) Oil.
    (B) Coolant.
    (C) Both of the above.
    (D) Neither of the above.

35. _____

36. Plate oil coolers are usually mounted _____.
    (A) in the engine
    (B) remotely
    (C) vertically
    (D) horizontally

36. _____

37. To clean the coolant section of a tube oil cooler, the
    cooling system should be _____.
    (A) evacuated
    (B) periodically reverse flushed
    (C) filled with special chemicals
    (D) brought up to operating temperatures

37. _____

38. If a tube oil cooler is disassembled for service, the cooling element should be checked for leaks by _____.
    (A) magnafluxing
    (B) dye-penetrant testing
    (C) ultraviolet testing
    (D) pressure testing

38. _____

39. Plate oil coolers should be checked for leaks by _____.
    (A) magnafluxing
    (B) dye-penetrant testing
    (C) ultraviolet testing
    (D) pressure testing

39. _____

40. The oil pressure relief valve stabilizes lubricating oil pressure at _____.
    (A) idle speeds
    (B) midrange speeds
    (C) high speeds
    (D) all speeds

40. _____

41. The oil pressure relief valve is held on its seat by _____.
    (A) oil pressure
    (B) spring pressure
    (C) centrifugal pressure
    (D) pneumatic pressure

41. _____

42. When oil pressure at the pressure relief valve exceeds approximately 50 psi (345 kPa), the valve _____.
    (A) seats
    (B) unseats
    (C) cycles
    (D) becomes dysfunctional

42. _____

43. List the two most common types of oil filters used on mobile diesel engines.

    _____

    _____

Name _____

44. To add strength to the cartridge oil filter and to help prevent damage during shipment and installation, the pleated element is usually surrounded by a(n) _____.

44. _____

    (A) metal body

    (B) chemical coating

    (C) centrifuge separator

    (D) coiled spring

45. Name three types of spin-on oil filters.

_____

_____

_____

46. The basic material used in surface filter elements is _____.

46. _____

    (A) cotton thread and supporting fibers

    (B) pleated paper

    (C) wire mesh

    (D) sintered copper strands

47. The basic material used in depth filter elements is _____.

47. _____

    (A) cotton thread and supporting fibers

    (B) pleated paper

    (C) wire mesh

    (D) sintered copper strands

48. The unit of measurement most commonly used to determine the degree of filtration of a filter element is the micron, which is approximately _____.

48. _____

    (A) .04″

    (B) .004″

    (C) .0004″

    (D) .00004″

49. List two major types of filtration systems used in modern diesel engines.

_____

_____

50. A bypass oil system only filters what approximate percentage of the circulating oil?

50. _____

    (A) 1%

    (B) 5%

    (C) 10%

    (D) 50%

51. Because 100% of the circulating oil must normally pass through a full-flow filtration system, which device prevents oil starvation to the engine in the event of filter blockage?
    (A) Bypass valve.
    (B) Pressure relief valve.
    (C) Poppet valve.
    (D) Desmodramic valve.

51. _____

52. Bypass valves are normally used with _____.
    (A) full-flow filtration systems
    (B) oil coolers
    (C) Both of the above.
    (D) Neither of the above.

52. _____

53. When draining the oil prior to replacing an oil filter, the oil should only be changed when it is _____.
    (A) cold
    (B) hot
    (C) bypassing
    (D) leaking

53. _____

54. When replacing oil filters, the rubber sealing ring should be installed _____.
    (A) on top of the old ring
    (B) only if the old ring was leaking
    (C) dry
    (D) only after being coated with clean engine oil

54. _____

Oil Pressure Indication Systems

55. The two most common systems used to warn the operator of low oil pressure situations are:

    _____

    _____

56. Occasionally, an oil pressure warning light will not go out after changing the oil and filter. What is the usual cause of this condition?
    (A) A stuck sensor.
    (B) Air entrapment.
    (C) Malfunctioning unit.
    (D) Electrical short.

56. _____

Name _____

57. The major component of a mechanical oil pressure
indicating system consists of a tube made of spring
metal and a pinion-and-sector mechanism referred to
as a(n) _____.

57. _____

   (A) bourdon tube gauge
   (B) reflux indicating gauge
   (C) coil-type gauge
   (D) electromagnetic gauge

58. What are the two major components of an electrical indicating system?

   _____

   _____

59. In an electromagnetic coil indicating system, oil
pressure works against the _____.

59. _____

   (A) slider
   (B) resistor
   (C) actuating lever
   (D) diaphragm

60. The type of oil gauge that uses two coils, each wound
around a bimetal strip is the _____.

60. _____

   (A) pressure switch indicating system
   (B) heating coil indicating system
   (C) electronic indicating system
   (D) electromagnetic coil indicating system

61. What is the major difference between the pressure switch indicating system and the other
gauge systems?

   _____

   _____

62. Although an electronic indicating system operates in
the same manner as the pressure switch system, it uses
a(n) _____ in place of the diaphragm.

62. _____

   (A) warning light
   (B) slider switch
   (C) wiper
   (D) relay assembly

63. The heated, fume-laden air must be vented from the   63. _____
    crankcase because _____.

    (A) the fumes are corrosive and will attack metal surfaces

    (B) the fumes will cause aeration in the lubricating oil

    (C) the fumes are combustible and could explode

    (D) the fumes are caustic and will attack gasket material

Engine Oils

64. To make the correct lubricating oil selection, there are three basic lubricating oil properties
    that should be understood. What are they?

    _____

    _____

    _____

65. API service classifications tell the user _____.   65. _____

    (A) the level of detergent in the oil

    (B) what type performance tests the oil has passed

    (C) the viscosity of the oil

    (D) the quality of the oil

66. When using the SAE oil viscosity classification system   66. _____
    to determine proper viscosity of oil, the thicker and
    heavier weight oils receive _____ numbers than the
    thinner or lighter weight oils.

    (A) higher

    (B) lower

    (C) more

    (D) fewer

67. A multi-viscosity oil with the rating of 10W-40 will   67. _____
    duplicate the properties of a 40-weight oil at _____.

    (A) 0°F

    (B) 0°C

    (C) 100°F

    (D) 100°C

68. An oil's TBN (total base number) measures its ability to   68. _____
    neutralize oil-borne _____.

    (A) bases

    (B) acids

    (C) contaminants

    (D) oxidants

Name _____

69. An oil's TAN (total acid number) measures the _____ of   69. _____
    the oil.
    (A) acidity
    (B) alkalinity
    (C) oxidant level
    (D) cold viscosity

70. The following are advantages of synthetic oils over   70. _____
    natural oils *except:*
    (A) temperature stability.
    (B) longevity.
    (C) better fuel economy.
    (D) quicker break-in time for new engines.

71. The best way to check engine oil contamination is   71. _____
    _____ _____.

Name _____

Date _____

Instructor _____

Score _____ Text pages 231–262

Chapter 11
Cooling Systems

After studying this chapter and completing supplemental exercises, you will be able to:

- Explain the purpose of a diesel engine cooling system.
- Describe the cooling system's basic components and explain their operation.
- Describe the difference between air and liquid cooling systems.
- Describe the major components of a diesel liquid cooling system.
- Explain how a thermostat regulates engine temperature.
- Explain why cooling system filters and conditioners are used.
- Describe coolant pump operation.
- Explain how an industrial diesel engine's heat exchanger works.
- Name the four types of cooling systems used with marine diesel engine applications.

Cooling Systems

1. Name the four ways in which heat is transferred from a diesel engine.

_____

_____

_____

_____

2. Name four problems that can occur if a diesel engine operates at a temperature below 150°F (65°C).

   _____

   _____

   _____

   _____

3. Name the two types of cooling systems used in diesel engines.

   _____

   _____

4. Technician A says air cooled systems are used on the majority of on-highway trucks. Technician B says numerous short cooling fins perform a better cooling job than a lesser number of large fins. Who is correct?

   (A) A only.

   (B) B only.

   (C) Both A & B.

   (D) Neither A nor B.

   4. _____

5. The liquid coolant used in liquid cooling systems is usually a mix of _____.

   (A) water and alcohol

   (B) water and ethylene glycol

   (C) water and benzene mentholane

   (D) Either A or B.

   5. _____

6. Technician A says engine coolant bypasses the radiator when the engine is cool. Technician B says the thermostat has two operating positions—completely open or closed. Who is correct?

   (A) A only.

   (B) B only.

   (C) Both A & B.

   (D) Neither A nor B.

   6. _____

7. On a closed cooling system, the water (coolant) pump pushes the coolant up through the _____ _____ surrounding the combustion chambers, where it can pick up heat from the engine.

   7. _____

8. Coolant flowing to the engine block is routed to three main areas. Name them.

   _____

   _____

   _____

Name _____

9. A(n) _____ assists the cooling process by controlling the flow of air through the shutters to the radiator.

    (A) thermostat

    (B) shutterstat

    (C) cooling solenoid

    (D) air relay

9. _____

10. Why shouldn't water alone be used in a cooling system?

_____

11. Technician A says that soluble oils are excellent corrosion inhibitors. Technician B says all corrosion inhibitors break down over time and must be replenished. Who is correct?

    (A) A only.

    (B) B only.

    (C) Both A & B.

    (D) Neither A nor B.

11. _____

12. Technician A says no coolant may be disposed of in septic tanks or streams, nor can it be dumped on the ground. Technician B says coolant must be solidified before it is sent to a landfill. Who is correct?

    (A) A only.

    (B) B only.

    (C) Both A & B.

    (D) Neither A nor B.

12. _____

13. List the two main purposes of a radiator.

_____

_____

14. A slight drop below the normal coolant level should not result in _____ of the coolant.

14. _____

15. In mobile applications, a surge or recovery tank would be best located _____ the radiator.

    (A) in front of

    (B) behind

    (C) above

    (D) below

15. _____

16. Coolant flow to and from the coolant recovery tank is controlled by valves located in the _____.
    (A) surge line
    (B) radiator cap
    (C) overflow line
    (D) recovery tank

16. _____

17. Name the two types of radiators found in mobile diesel applications.

_____

_____

18. Name the two types of flow patterns used in mobile diesel engine radiators.

_____

_____

19. Which describes low-flow radiator design?
    (A) Check ball to limit coolant flow to vent line.
    (B) Slower moving, cooler coolant flow.
    (C) Internal baffles to mix coolant.
    (D) All of the above.

19. _____

20. Technician A says that a 10-fin radiator core will cool more quickly than a 12-fin core, while Technician B says that the fan in the 12-fin core will need extra horsepower to operate efficiently. Who is correct?
    (A) A only.
    (B) B only.
    (C) Both A & B.
    (D) Neither A nor B.

20. _____

21. Excessive air in the coolant system can result in which of the following conditions?
    (A) Pump loses its prime.
    (B) Increase in corrosion.
    (C) Reduced overall capacity to dissipate heat.
    (D) All of the above.

21. _____

22. A(n) _____ _____ is placed around the cooling fan to increase the cooling efficiency of the radiator.

22. _____

Name _____

23. A radiator cap with a *9* stamped on it will allow _____ psi of pressure to build in the system before opening the atmospheric vent.

    (A) 9

    (B) 90

    (C) 19

    (D) None; caps are not stamped.

23. _____

24. The maximum coolant temperature allowed in the radiator regardless of the pressure cap used is _____.

    (A) 190°F

    (B) 200°F

    (C) 210°F

    (D) 220°F

24. _____

25. List the three major types of radiator shutter systems.

_____

_____

_____

Hoses

26. Technician A says the lower radiator hose is subject to the roughest service life of all cooling system hoses. Technician B says hoses normally wear from the inside out. Who is correct?

    (A) A only.

    (B) B only.

    (C) Both A & B.

    (D) Neither A nor B.

26. _____

27. List three indicators that a hose requires replacement.

_____

_____

_____

Cleaning and Replacing Cooling System Components

28. List five cooling system problems that can cause the engine to overheat.

_____

_____

_____

_____

_____

29. When replacing a radiator hose, Technician A cuts off the old hose and removes any remaining pieces with a wire brush. Technician B positions the hose clamp on top of the bead on the hose fitting nipple. Who is correct?

    (A) A only.

    (B) B only.

    (C) Both A & B.

    (D) Neither A nor B.

29. _____

30. Which of the following can be used to remove loose dirt and debris from the radiator core?

    (A) Spray gun.

    (B) Wire brush.

    (C) Air hose with a pressure nozzle.

    (D) All of the above.

30. _____

31. If the cooling system _____ is not maintained, overheating and loss of coolant can result.

31. _____

32. When leak-testing a radiator off a vehicle, pressurize the radiator with compressed air to _____ psi before submerging it in water.

    (A) 2–4

    (B) 7–10

    (C) 10–15

    (D) 20

32. _____

Name _____

33. Technician A says, if properly maintained, chemical
inhibitors can fully protect a cooling system.
Technician B says coolant filters are needed to remove
abrasive particles from the coolant flow. Who is
correct?

33. _____

(A) A only.

(B) B only.

(C) Both A & B.

(D) Neither A nor B.

34. Technician A says it is necessary to drain the coolant
system before changing the coolant filter. Technician B
says coolant filters are generally only used on bypass
type cooling systems. Who is correct?

34. _____

(A) A only.

(B) B only.

(C) Both A & B.

(D) Neither A nor B.

35. Most diesel engines are equipped with thermostats that
open in a temperature range of _____.

35. _____

(A) 150–170°F

(B) 170–195°F

(C) 195–210°F

(D) 210–220°F

36. A defective cooling system thermostat that _____ may
result in cold engine operation and/or incomplete
combustion of fuel.

36. _____

(A) is stuck open

(B) remains closed

(C) is partially opened

(D) All of the above.

37. Name two common problems that can damage a thermostat.

_____

_____

38. The heated water and ribbon test is used to check the
thermostat's _____ temperature rating.

38. _____

(A) starting

(B) start-to-open

(C) full-open

(D) None of the above.

39. The most important service consideration in any cooling system is keeping it _____.

39. _____

40. Technician A says that removal of the cooling system filler cap is not necessary when draining coolant from the system. Technician B says that after system drainage is complete, the drain cocks should be closed in freezing conditions. Who is correct?

    (A) A only.

    (B) B only.

    (C) Both A & B.

    (D) Neither A nor B.

40. _____

41. Technician A makes certain the heater shut-off valve is closed during the coolant refill operation. Technician B runs the engine with the radiator and recovery tank caps removed to help deaerate the freshly installed coolant. Who is correct?

    (A) A only.

    (B) B only.

    (C) Both A & B.

    (D) Neither A nor B.

41. _____

42. After using a scale remover as part of the flushing procedures, Technician A runs warm distilled water through the system. Technician B circulates a special neutralizing agent through the system and then reverse flushes it before filling with new coolant. Who is correct?

    (A) A only.

    (B) B only.

    (C) Both A & B.

    (D) Neither A nor B.

42. _____

43. A flushing gun uses _____ _____ to force flushing water back through the cooling system in a direction opposite of normal flow.

43. _____

Water Manifolds

44. What is the job of external water manifolds if they are used on some larger diesel engines?

_____

45. Coolant entering the water manifold leaves the cylinder head through openings directly over each _____ port.

45. _____

Name _____

Water Pumps

46. Name the two major designs of water pumps used in diesel cooling systems.

_____

_____

47. Label the major components of the centrifugal water pump illustrated.

(A) _____   (E) _____

(B) _____   (F) _____

(C) _____   (G) _____

(D) _____

48. The majority of coolant pump failures are caused by _____ in the pump.

48. _____

49. When is a water pump subject to thermal shock?

_____

V-Belt Drives

50. Name four reasons V-belt drive systems for water pumps are preferred over chains and gears.

_____

_____

_____

_____

51. What are the two major causes of belt slippage?

_____

_____

52. One of the major causes of engine overheating is _____ _____ _____.

52. _____

53. Normal deflection in a properly tensioned belt is in the range of _____.
    (A) 1/8″ to 1/4″
    (B) 3/8″ to 1/2″
    (C) 1/4″ to 3/4″
    (D) 1/2″ to 1″

53. _____

54. List the three major steps when checking a fan drive belt.

    _____

    _____

    _____

55. Name the two types of fan flow designs.

    _____

    _____

Suction Fans

56. The thermo-modulated fan assembly is one of the most popular designs of _____ type fans.

56. _____

Blower Fans

57. Technician A straightens bent fan blades during regular inspections and checks. Technician B replaces the fan if any blade is more the 3/32″ out of plane with the other blades. Who is correct?
    (A) A only.
    (B) B only.
    (C) Both A & B.
    (D) Neither A nor B.

57. _____

58. Name the two types of fan clutches.

    _____

    _____

59. Name the three types of coolant heaters used on diesel engines.

    _____

    _____

    _____

Name _____

Industrial Engine Cooling Systems

60. An industrial cooling system that removes heat by increasing the coolant temperature is known as a(n) _____ system.
    (A) ebullient
    (B) solid water
    (C) liquid water
    (D) emulsion

60. _____

61. An industrial cooling system that removes heat by changing water to steam is known as a(n) _____ system.
    (A) ebullient
    (B) solid water
    (C) liquid water
    (D) emulsion

61. _____

62. Name the three common components that remove heat in a solid water coolant system.

    _____

    _____

    _____

63. The need to meet environmental regulations and a high cost of operation are two disadvantages of a(n) _____.
    (A) cooling tower
    (B) surge tank
    (C) heat exchanger
    (D) radiator

63. _____

64. Name three functions of an expansion or surge tank in an industrial diesel engine cooling system.

    _____

    _____

    _____

65. Explain the difference between an expansion tank and a surge tank.

    _____

    _____

66. A(n) _____ in an expansion tank or expansion chamber
    of a surge tank allows for monitoring of the coolant
    level.

    66. _____

    (A) stop cock

    (B) expansion valve

    (C) sight glass

    (D) standpipe

67. Name three factors that can affect the exact pressure in an expansion tank of a cooling
    system.

    _____

    _____

    _____

68. Ebullient circulation is developed by coolant _____ at
    the hot surfaces in the engine.

    68. _____

    (A) condensing

    (B) vaporizing

    (C) circulating

    (D) leeching

69. Technician A says the steam pressure in a steam
    separator must be kept at a constant pressure to
    prevent overboiling. Technician B says a typical steam
    separator steam pressure is 150 psi at 250°F. Who is
    correct?

    69. _____

    (A) A only.

    (B) B only.

    (C) Both A & B.

    (D) Neither A nor B.

Marine Engine Cooling System

70. Name the four most popular engine cooling configurations used in marine diesel
    applications.

    _____

    _____

    _____

    _____

Name _____

71. In a raw-water cooling system, _____ is used as a coolant.
    (A) saltwater
    (B) freshwater
    (C) glycol based coolant
    (D) Either A or B.

71. _____

72. The closed cooling system of a marine engine actually consists of _____ circuit(s).

72. _____

73. One of the primary differences between a marine cooling system and a mobile installation is the use of a(n) _____ instead of a radiator.

73. _____

74. Name the three major designs of seawater cooling system pumps.

    _____

    _____

    _____

75. A centrifugal pump must be installed with the pump inlet _____.
    (A) above the light waterline of the boat
    (B) below the light waterline of the boat
    (C) perpendicular to the keel
    (D) None of the above.

75. _____

76. _____ must be installed in a marine cooling system to protect components from foreign materials in the seawater.

76. _____

77. In saltwater installations, scale and corrosive salts tend to build up in the _____ parts of the cooling system.
    (A) hottest
    (B) coolest
    (C) lowest
    (D) exposed

77. _____

78. To reduce the adverse effects of electrolysis in saltwater cooling systems, sacrificial _____ must be installed in the system.
    (A) iron anodes
    (B) zinc anodes
    (C) copper anodes
    (D) All of the above.

78. _____

79. _____ _____ cooling systems for marine applications   79. _____
combine the raw-water and conventional diesel engine
cooling systems into a single system.

80. Name the major components of a heat exchanger cooling system.

_____

_____

_____

81. Most inboard heat exchangers are _____ _____ _____   81. _____
type.

82. Name the major components of a keel cooling system.

_____

_____

_____

_____

83. When a radiator is used in a marine application,   83. _____
Technician A says engine exhaust gases must not be
drawn into the radiator. Technician B says the radiator
airflow should be opposite of the prevailing winds.
Who is correct?

(A) A only.

(B) B only.

(C) Both A & B.

(D) Neither A nor B.

Name _____

Date _____

Instructor _____

Score _____ Text pages 263–280

Chapter 12

Air Intake Systems

After studying this chapter and completing supplemental exercises, you will be able to:

- Explain the purpose and operation of diesel air intakes.
- Define scavenging and supercharging.
- Name the major air cleaner types and describe their operation.
- Explain the purpose of an air silencer.
- Describe the two principle types of blowers used in diesel air systems.

Air Intakes

1. List three adverse effects if the engine does not receive sufficient intake air.

_____

_____

_____

2. The ability of a four-cycle engine to fill a cylinder with clean fresh air is based on the engine's _____.

   (A) size

   (B) volumetric efficiency

   (C) cylinder diameter

   (D) mechanical efficiency

2. _____

3. If a cylinder that can hold 100 cubic inches of air has   3. _____
   80 cubic inches of air entering the cylinder under
   certain conditions, what is the volumetric efficiency?
   (A) 80%
   (B) 100%
   (C) 20%
   (D) 40%

4. Name three variables that can affect how well an engine breathes.

   _____

   _____

   _____

5. What unwanted condition can result from the valves of a four-cycle engine closing too soon?

   _____

   _____

6. Name the major components of an air intake system used on a naturally aspirated four-cycle
   engine.

   _____

   _____

   _____

   _____

Scavenging and Supercharging

7. _____ is the process by which air from the blower   7. _____
   clears the cylinder of combustion gases.
   (A) Supercharging
   (B) Turbocharging
   (C) Scavenging
   (D) Purging

8. Technician A says in a two-cycle engine scavenging   8. _____
   takes place during the end of the downstroke
   (expansion) and the beginning of the upstroke
   (compression). Technician B says scavenging air has
   very little effect on cooling the engine. Who is correct?
   (A) A only.
   (B) B only.
   (C) Both A & B.
   (D) Neither A nor B.

Name _____

9. _____ is a process that supplies more air to the intake system than is normally taken in under atmospheric pressures.

9. _____

10. Identify the three methods of scavenging shown in the illustration.

(A) _____

(B) _____

(C) _____

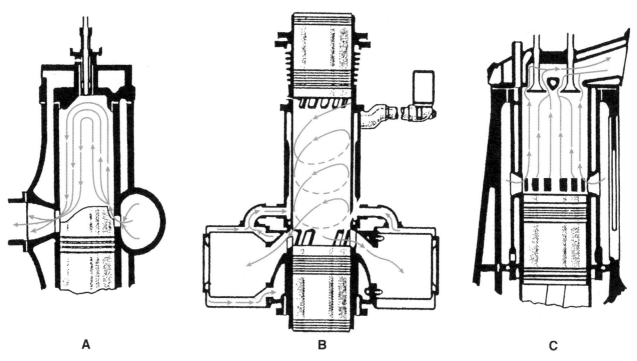

      A   **B**   **C**

11. The increase in air pressure generated by supercharging with a blower is generally in the range of _____.

11. _____

(A) 0–1 psi

(B) 1–5 psi

(C) 5–7 psi

(D) 7–10 psi

12. Technician A says there is no difference in the valve timing of a supercharged four-cycle engine versus a non-supercharged four-cycle engine. Technician B says that with a supercharged four-cycle engine the intake valve opening is advanced and the exhaust valve closing is retarded. Who is correct?

12. _____

(A) A only.

(B) B only.

(C) Both A & B.

(D) Neither A nor B.

13. In a(n) _____-cycle engine, both scavenging and supercharging take place while the piston is in the lower part of the cylinder.

13. _____

Air Cleaners

14. Name four problems contaminants in the combustion air may cause.

_____

_____

_____

_____

15. Name four common airborne contaminants.

_____

_____

_____

_____

16. A plugged or dirty air filter can cause _____ fuel burning.

16. _____

17. _____ in the air duct leading from the filter provide paths for dirt to get in the engine.

17. _____

18. Identify the components of the precleaner and prescreener assembly.

(A) _____

(B) _____

(C) _____

(D) _____

(E) _____

(F) _____

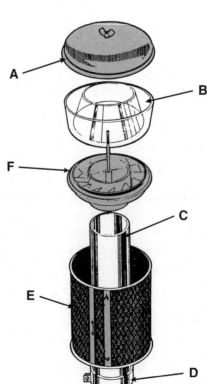

Name _____

19. Name two simple systems that can be used to reduce water problems in the air intake system.

_____

_____

20. Name three types of moisture separators used to remove moisture from the air in the air inlet system.

_____

_____

_____

Intake Air Cleaners

21. Name the two basic types of air cleaners used in diesel engines.

_____

_____

22. Identify the major components of an oil bath air cleaner.

(A) _____   (D) _____

(B) _____   (E) _____

(C) _____

23. List the three steps in servicing an oil bath air cleaner.

_____

_____

_____

24. _____ air cleaners are commonly used for on-highway diesel trucks and vehicles.

24. _____

25. Heavy-duty dry air filters have a minimum efficiency rating of _____ %.
    (A) 99
    (B) 99.9
    (C) 99.99
    (D) 100

25. _____

26. Identify the components of the two-stage dry air filter.
    (A) _____
    (B) _____
    (C) _____
    (D) _____
    (E) _____
    (F) _____
    (G) _____

27. In extremely severe operating environments, a(n) _____ _____ may be used inside the primary air filter to prevent dirt from entering the engine during installation and removal of the filter.

27. _____

28. _____ air filters are popular intake air filters for farm equipment.
    (A) Multi-tube
    (B) Panel
    (C) Spiral rotor
    (D) Concave tube

28. _____

Name _____

29. List three methods of determining air cleaner service intervals.

_____

_____

_____

30. A(n) _____ _____ is a test instrument that can be used to measure air inlet restriction.

30. _____

31. When checking air inlet restriction on a turbocharged engine, Technician A connects the manometer downstream of the turbocharger inlet. Technician B allows the engine to run under full load before taking the reading. Who is correct?

(A) A only.

(B) B only.

(C) Both A & B.

(D) Neither A nor B.

31. _____

32. When checking air inlet restriction, a good rule of thumb is not to exceed _____ inches of water on the manometer.

(A) 5

(B) 10

(C) 15

(D) 20

32. _____

33. The vacuator valve is often incorrectly left open when a service technician performs what procedure?

33. _____

_____

34. Unless it is specifically checked for, name three situations that can cause a low air restriction reading that is very difficult to identify.

_____

_____

_____

Changing Air Filter Elements

35. List three problems with gaskets on new filter elements that can lead to air leaks.

_____

_____

_____

Intake Air Silencers

36. The rush of high volumes of air into the air cleaners
often require that the cleaner be equipped with a(n)
_____.

    (A) venturi

    (B) air silencer

    (C) screen mesh cap

    (D) positive displacement blower

36. _____

37. At what point in the air intake system should the air silencer be installed?

_____

Blowers

38. Blowers deliver large volumes of air at pressures _____.

    (A) below 1 psi

    (B) between 1 and 5 psi

    (C) at atmospheric pressure

    (D) above 5 psi

38. _____

39. Name the two basic blower designs.

_____

_____

Positive Displacement Blowers

40. Name the main advantage of a Roots blower.

_____

41. What is the normal operating speed of a Roots blower?

    (A) 1000–2000 rpm

    (B) 2000–4000 rpm

    (C) 2000–6000 rpm

    (D) 6000–9000 rpm

41. _____

42. A(n) _____ blower takes its power from the exhaust gas
of the engine.

42. _____

Name _____

Intake Air Passages

43. In two-cycle engines, the passage that conducts intake   43. _____
    air to the cylinders is generally called a(n) _____ _____.

44. Technician A says air box drains are never vented   44. _____
    to the atmosphere for environmental reasons.
    Technician B says drains are especially important
    when the air cooler is installed between the blower
    discharge and the air intake manifold or receiver.
    Who is correct?
    (A) A only.
    (B) B only.
    (C) Both A & B.
    (D) Neither A nor B.

45. Frontal air intake systems used on on-highway trucks can lead to what particular problem?

    _____

46. Because of the _____ generated behind a truck's air   46. _____
    deflector, the concentration of moisture there may be
    higher than at a frontal air intake.

47. Technician A says air passages may or may not be   47. _____
    an integral part of a four-cycle diesel engine block.
    Technician B says external intake manifolds are often
    more difficult to remove and service than integral
    manifolds. Who is correct?
    (A) A only.
    (B) B only.
    (C) Both A & B.
    (D) Neither A nor B.

48. When sealing the intake manifold to the engine block,   48. _____
    the technician should _____.
    (A) reuse the gasket if it is in good condition
    (B) take maximum advantage of the available bolt
        torque
    (C) avoid the use of adhesives to hold the gasket in
        place
    (D) All of the above.

49. Some diesel engines have a(n) _____ _____ _____   49. _____
    to stop the engine whenever abnormal operating
    conditions are encountered.

50. The air shutdown housing is normally mounted _____.   50. _____

    (A) on the side of the intake manifold

    (B) on the side of the blower

    (C) near the turbocharger

    (D) on the exhaust manifold

Name _____

Date _____

Instructor _____

Score _____ Text pages 281–306

Chapter 13

Exhaust Systems

After studying this chapter and completing supplemental exercises, you will be able to:

- Explain the purpose of exhaust systems used on diesel engines.
- List the main components of a typical exhaust system.
- Name some of the more common diesel engine emission controls.
- Explain the purpose of an EGR system
- Explain the purpose of a diesel after treatment system.
- Define back pressure and describe its effect on the exhaust system.
- Understand the precautions that must be taken when routing exhaust pipes.
- Describe the parts and operation of a turbocharger.
- Explain the purpose of charge air coolers.
- Identify the causes of turbocharger failure.
- Explain the operation of an exhaust pyrometer.

Exhaust System

1. Name the main components used in a mobile diesel engine application, such as a heavy-duty truck.

_____

_____

_____

_____

2. On most mobile diesel engines, a(n) _____ is installed in the exhaust system and is driven by exhaust gases.

2. _____

3. List three sources of resistance in an exhaust system that can create unwanted back pressure.

_____

_____. _____

_____

4. Technician A says excessive back pressure can lead to loss of power. Technician B says low back pressure results in better fuel economy at any engine speed. Who is correct?

4. _____

   (A) A only.
   (B) B only.
   (C) Both A & B.
   (D) Neither A nor B.

Exhaust System Components

5. The _____ _____ collects engine exhaust gases from the cylinder ports and carries them to an exhaust pipe.

5. _____

6. If exhaust gases remain in the cylinder after the exhaust stroke, what two problems can occur?

_____

_____

7. On marine applications, most exposed surfaces of the exhaust manifold are _____ with spin glass.

7. _____

8. When servicing an exhaust manifold, Technician A allows the manifold to cool before removing it from the block. Technician B cleans all carbon and metal chips from the inside of the manifold. Who is correct?

8. _____

   (A) A only.
   (B) B only.
   (C) Both A & B.
   (D) Neither A nor B.

9. When checking the manifold with a straightedge, the maximum allowable clearance (warpage) between the straightedge and manifold is normally _____.

9. _____

   (A) .002″ (.05 mm)
   (B) .004″ (.1 mm)
   (C) .006″ (.15 mm)
   (D) .008″ (.2 mm)

Name _____

10. A(n) _____ is used to prevent leakage between the mating surfaces of the engine and the exhaust manifold.

10. _____

11. Technician A cleans the mating surfaces before installing a new exhaust manifold gasket. Technician B torques the mounting bolts in the proper sequence and retorques them after engine warm up. Who is correct?
    (A) A only.
    (B) B only.
    (C) Both A & B.
    (D) Neither A nor B.

11. _____

12. Name two major designs of mufflers.

_____

_____

_____

13. Which type of muffler is also known as a reverse-flow muffler?

_____

14. In both wet and dry mufflers used in marine applications, _____ _____ is used to cool the exhaust gases.

14. _____

15. Mufflers used on engines equipped with turbochargers are _____.
    (A) more complex in design
    (B) simpler in design
    (C) located after the turbocharger in the exhaust flow
    (D) Both B & C.

15. _____

16. In addition to acting as silencers, most mufflers also function as _____ _____.

16. _____

17. Relatively low exhaust gas temperatures in newer engines allow more _____ to remain in the exhaust system, which can lead to corrosion.

17. _____

18. On some mobile diesel applications, a second muffler known as a(n) _____ is used to further reduce exhaust noise.

18. _____

19. Technician A says silencers are usually required on exhaust systems with turbochargers due to the increased noise of the turbocharger. Technician B says it is best to place the silencer or muffler as close as possible to the engine in industrial applications to reduce interference caused by the pulsating effect of the engine. Who is correct?

(A) A only.

(B) B only.

(C) Both A & B.

(D) Neither A nor B.

19. _____

20. _____ engine blocks are usually equipped with separate exhaust systems for each bank of cylinders.

20. _____

21. List two drawbacks of vertical muffler systems used in mobile applications.

_____

_____

22. List two drawbacks of horizontal muffler systems used in mobile applications.

_____

_____

23. Technician A says dual stack exhaust systems on mobile applications can reduce back pressure and increase fuel economy. Technician B says dual stack systems are more effective on larger engine sizes. Who is correct?

(A) A only.

(B) B only.

(C) Both A & B.

(D) Neither A nor B.

23. _____

24. What is the purpose of selective catalytic reduction?

_____

_____

_____

25. Name three materials used for exhaust pipes that can withstand the heat demands of the system.

_____

_____

_____

26. In industrial exhaust systems, hangers must allow for _____ _____ of the pipe.

26. _____

27. Name three major characteristics of a wet exhaust system used in marine applications.

_____

_____

_____

Name _____

28. Technician A says that NO_x pollutants are formed
    during lean combustion. Technician B says most EGR
    systems precool the exhaust gas before introducing it
    into the intake system. Who is correct?

    (A) A only.

    (B) B only.

    (C) Both A & B.

    (D) Neither A nor B.

28. _____

29. EGR systems decrease the amount of useable _____
    in the cylinder, thereby reducing the amount of NO_x
    pollutants produced.

29. _____

30. List and briefly describe the two regeneration methods used with different diesel
    particulate filters.

    _____

    _____

    _____

31. _____ _____ _____ separates nitrogen from oxygen in order to reduce NO_x emissions.

    _____

32. Diesel exhaust fluid (DEF) is a 32% solution of
    _____ and water.

32. _____

33. Technician A says that a diesel/water emulsion system
    mixes water with diesel fuel before it is injected into
    the cylinders. Technician B says that diesel/water
    emulsion increases the temperature in the combustion
    chamber. Who is correct?

    (A) A only.

    (B) B only.

    (C) Both A & B.

    (D) Neither A nor B.

33. _____

Exhaust System Service

34. What are three problems that can be caused by partial restrictions or blockages in the
    exhaust system?

    _____

    _____

    _____

35. Name four major sources of noise generation in on-highway truck applications.

_____

_____

_____

_____

Turbochargers

36. What is the job of a turbocharger in a diesel engine?

_____

37. Technician A says turbochargers are not used on two-cycle engines. Technician B says turbochargers increase an engine's fuel economy. Who is correct?

37. _____

(A) A only.

(B) B only.

(C) Both A & B.

(D) Neither A nor B.

38. Name the components of the turbocharger shown in the illustration below.

(A) _____   (D) _____

(B) _____   (E) _____

(C) _____   (F) _____

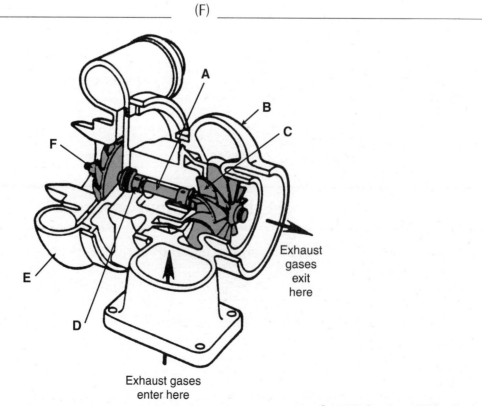

Exhaust gases exit here

Exhaust gases enter here

Name _____

39. The _____ _____ delivers the fresh compressed air
from the turbocharger to the intake manifold.

39. _____

40. Technician A says one problem with turbochargers
is that they cannot react to the changing demands of
the engine. Technician B says turbochargers can help
engines perform well at high altitudes. Who is correct?

(A) A only.

(B) B only.

(C) Both A & B.

(D) Neither A nor B.

40. _____

41. A(n) _____ _____ turbocharger varies the amount of
exhaust gas used to drive the turbine wheel, which
varies the output of the compressor.

41. _____

42. Name two common problems whose symptoms are often mistaken for turbocharger
problems.

_____

_____

43. List three common symptoms of turbocharger problems.

_____

_____

_____

44. Name the first two steps in troubleshooting turbocharger problems.

_____

_____

45. _____ smoke is a sign of engine oil consumption.

45. _____

Charge Air Coolers

46. Name three advantages of cooling air before introducing it into the combustion chamber.

_____

_____

_____

47. Name the two types of charge air coolers currently in use.

_____

_____

Exhaust Pyrometers

48. Exhaust pyrometers are used to measure the _____ of   48. _____
the exhaust gases in each cylinder.

Exhaust Brakes

49. An exhaust brake _____ the service brakes on diesel-   49. _____
powered vehicles.

Alternative Fuels

50. List four alternative fuels that generate fewer pollutants than diesel fuel.

_____

_____

_____

_____

Name _____

Date _____

Instructor _____

Score _____ Text pages 307–320

Chapter 14
Diesel Fuels

After studying this chapter and completing supplemental exercises, you will be able to:

- Explain diesel fuel grades.
- Discuss fuel properties and characteristics.
- Explain the reason for the use of fuel additives.
- Describe the proper procedures for handling and storage of diesel fuel.
- Name the various alternative fuels and their properties.

Hydrocarbon Fuels

1. Crude oil compounds such as benzene, petane, hexane, heptane, and propane are all examples of _____.

   (A) complex compounds

   (B) elements

   (C) hydrocarbons

   (D) inert gases

1. _____

2. Each crude oil compound will have its own _____ _____ point because it will vaporize or flash at its own distinct temperature.

2. _____

3. The first hydrocarbon fuel obtained from crude oil is
   _____.
   (A) diesel fuel
   (B) kerosene
   (C) aviation fuel
   (D) gasoline

3. _____

4. Name the process when crude oil is heated to obtain
   its various hydrocarbons.
   (A) Purification.
   (B) Distillation.
   (C) Dehydration.
   (D) None of the above.

4. _____

Diesel Fuel Grades

5. Which diesel fuel grades are considered acceptable for
   use in high-speed trucks and buses in North America?
   (A) Grades 1D and 2D.
   (B) Grades 3D and 4D.
   (C) Grades 1 D, 2D, 3D, and 4D.
   (D) Grades 2D and 3D.

5. _____

6. Which grade of fuel is the premium fuel used in
   high rpm engines requiring frequent load and speed
   changes?
   (A) Grade 4D.
   (B) Grade 3D.
   (C) Grade 2D.
   (D) Grade 1D.

6. _____

7. Technician A says using the improper grade of fuel
   can affect engine performance. Technician B says
   additives are one way of beating cold starting problems
   associated with heavier diesel fuel grades. Who is
   correct?
   (A) A only.
   (B) B only.
   (C) Both A & B.
   (D) Neither A nor B.

7. _____

Name _____

8. List five properties of diesel fuel that affect diesel engine performance.

_____

_____

_____

_____

_____

9. A(n) _____ is used to test the heat value of a diesel fuel.

9. _____

10. Technician A says a Btu is the amount of heat needed to raise the temperature of one pound of water 10°F while Technician B adds that the metric equivalent of a Btu is a joule. Who is correct?

10. _____

   (A) A only.
   (B) B only.
   (C) Both A & B.
   (D) Neither A nor B.

11. Technician A says a fuel's flash point typically indicates the way it will ignite within an engine cylinder while Technician B adds that a fuel oil with an extremely low flash point can be dangerous to store and handle. Who is correct?

11. _____

   (A) A only.
   (B) B only.
   (C) Both A & B.
   (D) Neither A nor B.

12. _____ refers to the ability of a liquid fuel to vaporize and ignite easily in the combustion chamber without flame or spark.

12. _____

   (A) Flash point
   (B) Volatility
   (C) Ignition quality
   (D) None of the above.

13. The _____ is based on the ability of the diesel fuel to ignite.

13. _____

   (A) octane number
   (B) cetane number
   (C) viscosity rating
   (D) cloud point

14. According to the cetane number rating scale, the highest possible rating for a quality diesel fuel would be _____.

14. _____

15. Most cetane improvers contain _____.
    (A) hydrocarbons
    (B) alkyl nitrates
    (C) kerosene
    (D) alcohol

15. _____

16. A typical cetane improver will typically increase the cetane rating _____.
    (A) 1 to 3 numbers
    (B) 3 to 5 numbers
    (C) 5 to 10 numbers
    (D) Not at all.

16. _____

17. The higher the cetane number, the shorter the _____ _____.

17. _____

18. A fuel's cloud point should typically be at least _____ below ambient temperature to obtain satisfactory engine performance.
    (A) 5°F
    (B) 10°F
    (C) 15°F
    (D) 20°F

18. _____

19. Grade 2D diesel fuel has a cloud point of _____.
    (A) 0°F
    (B) 10°F
    (C) –10°F
    (D) –20°F

19. _____

20. Grade 1D diesel fuel has a cloud point of _____.
    (A) 0°F
    (B) 10°F
    (C) –10°F
    (D) –20°F

20. _____

Name _____

21. One of the most effective chemical methods for
lowering a fuel's cloud point is by blending a #2 fuel
with _____.

    (A) a #3 fuel

    (B) additives

    (C) kerosene

    (D) All of the above.

21. _____

22. _____ is the property of a diesel fuel that resists the
force that causes the fluid to flow.

22. _____

23. What are two common testing methods used to measure a fuel's viscosity?

_____

_____

24. Technician A says a diesel fuel's viscosity will change
with temperature. Technician B says diesel fuel with
a very low viscosity will result in coarse or heavy fuel
atomization. Who is correct?

    (A) A only.

    (B) B only.

    (C) Both A & B.

    (D) Neither A nor B.

24. _____

25. Which of the following fuel characteristics is *not*
affected by its viscosity?

    (A) Lubrication.

    (B) Atomization.

    (C) Ignition.

    (D) Heat value.

25. _____

26. _____ _____ is the deposit remaining in the fuel
chamber when there is incomplete combustion or
where a residual blend fuel has been used.

26. _____

27. Standard specifications allow for a maximum of
_____% soot ash content.

    (A) .001

    (B) .002

    (C) .01

    (D) .02

27. _____

28. Name three conditions that can occur as a result of a high sulfur content in a diesel fuel.

_____

_____

_____

29. Technician A says regulations state a diesel fuel should have a sulfur content of no more than .35% by weight with a maximum aromatic content of 5% while Technician B says even non-highway diesel engines are required to use ultra-low sulfur diesel fuel. Who is correct?

    (A) A only.

    (B) B only.

    (C) Both A & B.

    (D) Neither A nor B.

29. _____

30. Sulfur is removed from a diesel fuel by a process called _____.

30. _____

31. _____ are the two most common hydrocarbon utilizing microorganisms found in diesel fuel.

    (A) Corrosion and bacteria

    (B) Fungus and bacteria

    (C) Corrosion and fungus

    (D) None of the above.

31. _____

32. _____ is the most common form of diesel fuel contaminant.

    (A) Dirt

    (B) Water

    (C) Corrosion

    (D) Fungus

32. _____

33. Name the two types of water contamination in diesel fuel.

    _____

    _____

Fuel Additives

34. Name three diesel fuel characteristics that can be improved through the use of fuel additives.

    _____

    _____

    _____

Name _____

Fuel Handling and Storage

35. Any air, sediment (dirt), or water that enters the   35. _____
    diesel fuel system is commonly referred to as a(n)
    _____ material.

36. Which of the following materials is *not* recommended   36. _____
    in diesel fuel storage tank construction?
    (A) Fiberglass.
    (B) Steel.
    (C) Copper.
    (D) All of the above.

37. Who typically regulates the size specifications for   37. _____
    diesel fuel storage tanks?
    (A) Bureau of Fire Underwriters.
    (B) American Petroleum Institute.
    (C) American Society of Testing Materials.
    (D) None of the above.

Alternative Fuels

38. Why is compressed natural gas not currently used on diesel trucks, even though it has been
    used to fuel city buses?

    _____

39. Technician A says that alcohol-based fuel is desirable   39. _____
    because it need not be manufactured from crude oil
    while Technician B adds that ethyl alcohol and methyl
    alcohol are the two most common types of alcohol-
    based fuels. Who is correct?
    (A) A only.
    (B) B only.
    (C) Both A & B.
    (D) Neither A nor B.

40. A(n) _____ fuel can be manufactured using soybeans,   40. _____
    processed animal fats, or cooking oils.

2. Label the major components of a diesel engine fuel system.

(A) _____   (D) _____

(B) _____   (E) _____

(C) _____

Return fuel line

A

E

B

C

D

High pressure
Medium pressure
Gravity pressure
No pressure

Fuel supply line   Fuel tank

3. Fuel is pulled from the fuel tank by the _____ _____
   _____.

3. _____

4. Fuel lines from the fuel tank to the transfer pump and
   from the transfer pump to the fuel injection pump
   operate under _____ pressures.
   (A) low to moderate
   (B) moderate to high
   (C) high
   (D) atmospheric

4. _____

5. The various components of the low-pressure fuel
   delivery system should be _____.
   (A) kept away from engine heat
   (B) located above electrical equipment
   (C) easily accessible for servicing
   (D) All of the above.

5. _____

6. In some cases, a(n) _____ _____ fuel delivery system
   can eliminate the need for a fuel transfer pump.

6. _____

7. Sedimenters or agglomerator filters should be located
   on the _____ side of the transfer pump.

7. _____

Name _____

8. A(n) _____ _____ should be located before the first point at which wax could cause a restriction, typically the primary fuel filter.

8. _____

Fuel Tanks

9. Technician A says that diesel fuel tanks also function as cooling tanks for fuel returning from the injectors. Technician B says that in most cases, a fuel tank can be altered to fit the available space. Who is correct?

   (A) A only.

   (B) B only.

   (C) Both A & B.

   (D) Neither A nor B.

9. _____

10. The fuel tank on a highway vehicle is being discussed. Technician A says the tank must not extend beyond the vehicle's body. Technician B says the tank must be mounted high enough to gravity feed the injectors. Who is correct?

    (A) A only.

    (B) B only.

    (C) Both A & B.

    (D) Neither A nor B.

10. _____

11. Technician A says that galvanized steel fuel tanks are a strong economical choice for on-highway mobile applications. Technician B says steel tanks are heavy but extremely strong for off-highway applications. Who is correct?

    (A) A only.

    (B) B only.

    (C) Both A & B.

    (D) Neither A nor B.

11. _____

12. When properly designed and constructed, the holes in a baffle plate should be large enough to allow for proper fuel flow but small enough to prevent the fuel from _____ when the truck is moving.

12. _____

13. The bottom of the fuel tank _____.   13. _____
  (A) should be angled to collect contaminants at its
     lowest point
  (B) should have a drain port
  (C) should be ribbed for strength
  (D) Both A & B.

14. Most diesel engine manufacturers recommend that   14. _____
  the fuel tank be drained _____ to remove water
  (A) at least once a month
  (B) at least once a year
  (C) once every eighteen months
  (D) once every two years

15. Diesel fuel weighs up to _____ pounds per gallon.   15. _____
  (A) 5
  (B) 7.5
  (C) 10
  (D) 12

16. On average, _____ % of the fuel flowing through the   16. _____
  injectors returns to the fuel tank.
  (A) 90
  (B) 85
  (C) 80
  (D) 75

17. Why is a 5% expansion space required within a diesel fuel tank?

_____

18. Name two ways air bubbles can form in the fuel inside a fuel tank.

_____

_____

19. Which condition results from proper ventilation?   19. _____
  (A) Less clogging.
  (B) Less dirt and air in the system.
  (C) Greater fuel flow.
  (D) All of the above.

Name _____

20. Technician A says the fuel pickup or suction tube should be positioned near the drain plug of the fuel tank and at least 1″ up from the tank bottom. Technician B says the tube should be equipped with a gauze type filter. Who is correct?

   (A) A only.

   (B) B only.

   (C) Both A & B.

   (D) Neither A nor B.

20. _____

21. Technician A says the fuel tank should have a raised filler neck to prevent the entry of water. Technician B says gauze type filter screens should never be installed in the tank's filler neck. Who is correct?

   (A) A only.

   (B) B only.

   (C) Both A & B.

   (D) Neither A nor B.

21. _____

22. When no other means of ventilation is present, the tank's _____ _____ must be designed to allow air to enter the tank so fuel can flow easily.

22. _____

23. How many diesel fuel tanks are found on most heavy-duty highway vehicles?

23. _____

24. Which of the following statements applies to a fuel tank with an equalizer line built into it?

   (A) The equalizer line eliminates the need for a manual switch.

   (B) The fuel can settle to uneven levels.

   (C) Each tank is filled from a different opening.

   (D) All of the above.

24. _____

25. In industrial applications where the fuel tank is positioned above the injectors, name two methods of preventing hydrostatic lock.

   _____

   _____

26. _____ trapped in the fuel lines can prevent fuel from being picked up during starting.

26. _____

27. Name the three basic types of electric fuel gauges used in diesel powered vehicles.

   _____

   _____

   _____

28. The _____ fuel gauge system has two blades, each with a heating coil connected in series through the ignition switch to the battery.

    (A) balancing coil

    (B) thermostatic

    (C) vacuum

    (D) digital

28. _____

29. Which of the following gauge systems requires the use of a sensor, computer, and display unit?

    (A) Digital.

    (B) Analog.

    (C) Vacuum.

    (D) None of the above.

29. _____

Fuel Lines

30. Name the three types or grades of fuel lines currently used on diesel engines.

    _____

    _____

    _____

31. Fuel line replacement is being discussed. Technician A says that 5/8″ outside diameter steel tubing is suitable for high-pressure lines in most mobile applications. Technician B says that flexible sections of fuel line are often required in stationary applications. Who is correct?

    (A) A only.

    (B) B only.

    (C) Both A & B.

    (D) Neither A nor B.

31. _____

32. Technician A says that heavyweight steel tubing can be copper-coated to reduce the possibility of corrosion. Technician B says that when replacing a tube, the new tubing should be identical in appearance to the old tubing. Who is correct?

    (A) A only.

    (B) B only.

    (C) Both A & B.

    (D) Neither A nor B.

32. _____

Name _____

33. Why is copper tubing not recommended in a diesel installation?

_____

34. Steel tubing fuel lines are joined using _____
connections.

34. _____

35. Label the major components of a flared connection.

(A) _____

(B) _____

36. A medium-weight hose should be able to handle the
following amount of pressure safely.

(A) 200 psi

(B) 250 psi

(C) 300 psi

(D) 350 psi

36. _____

37. If the _____ _____ lines are too small in diameter,
pressuring inside the fuel injectors can rise, decreasing
engine efficiency.

37. _____

38. Low- or non-pressure fuel lines may be constructed
from which of the following materials?

(A) Mylar hose.

(B) Steel tubing.

(C) Neoprene hose.

(D) All of the above.

38. _____

39. When the fuel tank is located a considerable distance
from the engine, the _____ _____ diameter may need
to be increased to overcome fuel flow resistance.

39. _____

40. A suction line restriction reading indicates the amount
of _____ required to pull fuel into the pump.

40. _____

41. Technician A recommends all pipe and tapered threads on newly installed fuel lines be coated with an approved sealant. Technician B adds that new fuel lines must have the ability to move and flex with the chassis to prevent damage. Who is correct?

(A) A only.

(B) B only.

(C) Both A & B.

(D) Neither A nor B.

41. _____

42. Describe the proper method of tightening a flared connection.

_____

_____

Fuel Transfer Pumps (Supply Pumps)

43. The diesel technician can use the _____ lever to manually prime or purge all air from the system before starting the engine.

(A) hand-purge

(B) diaphragm

(C) hand-prime

(D) None of the above.

43. _____

44. Which of the following components is not typically found in a mechanically-operated diaphragm transfer pump?

(A) Spring-loaded diaphragm.

(B) Actuator arm

(C) Outlet valve.

(D) Plunger.

44. _____

45. The electric diaphragm transfer pump has a flexible metal bellows that is operated by a(n) _____.

45. _____

46. A plunger transfer pump has a(n) _____ on the injection pump camshaft that actuates the pump's plunger.

46. _____

47. The _____ transfer pump is a positive-displacement pump that is typically driven directly from the end of the governor shaft.

47. _____

Name _____

48. When inspecting and cleaning, the technician can check the weep hole for leaks in which of the following transfer pumps?

    (A) Gear fuel.

    (B) Piston fuel.

    (C) Diaphragm.

    (D) None of the above.

48. _____

49. When rebuilding a _____ transfer pump, the technician should make sure check valves are installed to open in the direction of fuel flow.

    (A) gear fuel

    (B) piston fuel

    (C) diaphragm

    (D) None of the above.

49. _____

50. When servicing a gear transfer pump, Technician A cleans up a lightly scored relief valve using an emery cloth. Technician B discards the pump drive assembly after finding worn bearings. Who is correct?

    (A) A only.

    (B) B only.

    (C) Both A & B.

    (D) Neither A nor B.

50. _____

Name _____

Date _____

Instructor _____

Score _____ Text pages 337–348

Chapter 16

Fuel Filters and Conditioners

After studying this chapter and completing supplemental exercises, you will be able to:

- Explain the importance of fuel filters.
- Name several types of fuel filters.
- Describe the various fuel filtration systems.
- Change both bolt-on and spin-on fuel filters.
- Explain the purpose of major types of diesel fuel conditioners.

Damage by Dirt and Water

1. Dirt particles in diesel fuel systems do not have to be very large to cause substantial damage. Most contaminants are measured in units called microns. How large is a micron?

    (A) 1/1000 (.001) of an inch.

    (B) 1/1000 (.001) of a meter.

    (C) 1/1000 (.001) of a yard.

    (D) 1/1000 (.001) of a millimeter.

1. _____

2. Abrasive dirt particles that range in size from _____   2. _____
   microns are the most damaging to diesel fuel systems.
   (A) 1–5
   (B) 5–20
   (C) 20–50
   (D) 50–200

3. Gasoline gives off a vapor barrier that keeps water out.   3. _____
   Diesel fuel _____.
   (A) gives off a similar vapor barrier that keeps water out
   (B) does not easily absorb water
   (C) will not mix with water
   (D) will easily absorb water

4. To minimize water in the fuel supply, many fleet owners   4. _____
   require that equipment fuel tanks be filled _____.
   (A) first thing in the morning
   (B) before the tank level falls below 1/2 full
   (C) before the tank level falls below 1/4 full
   (D) at the end of the day

Filtration Devices

5. The type of filtration device that collects large dirt   5. _____
   particles and water droplets by precipitating them out
   of the fuel is called a(n) _____.
   (A) sedimenter
   (B) agglomerator
   (C) final filter
   (D) water treatment filter

6. The type of filtration device that combines water   6. _____
   separation and collection with efficient fuel filtration is
   called a(n) _____.
   (A) sedimenter
   (B) agglomerator
   (C) final filter
   (D) water treatment filter

Name _____

7. The contaminants collected in the base of a prefilter unit are periodically removed by _____.

  (A) changing the filter element

  (B) draining off the contaminants through a drain cock

  (C) adding a water dispersant fuel treatment to the fuel tank

  (D) reverse flushing the filtration system

7. _____

8. When a prefilter is used primarily for water removal, it should be located _____.

  (A) between the filler spout and the tank

  (B) between the tank and the transfer pump

  (C) between the secondary filter and the injector pump

  (D) between the fuel return outlet and the fuel tank

8. _____

9. The size of impurities that can be removed by a filter is determined by _____.

  (A) the porosity of the filtering material

  (B) the rate of fuel flow

  (C) the distance of the filter from the tank

  (D) the temperature of the fuel being filtered

9. _____

10. Depth fuel filter elements are generally made of _____.

  (A) sintered metal strands

  (B) mechanical centrifuge diaphragm

  (C) pleated paper made of processed cellulose fibers

  (D) woven cotton sock material

10. _____

11. Surface filter elements are generally made of _____.

  (A) sintered metal strands

  (B) mechanical centrifuge diaphragm

  (C) pleated paper made of processed cellulose fibers

  (D) woven cotton sock material

11. _____

12. Many diesel engines are equipped with a two-stage filtration system that contains a primary and a secondary filter. These filters are _____.

  (A) not interchangeable

  (B) usually marked *P* and *S* to differentiate them

  (C) Both of the above.

  (D) Neither of the above.

12. _____

13. The primary filter is generally installed _____.   13. _____
    (A) between the fuel tank and the transfer pump
    (B) between the fuel transfer pump and the injector
        pump
    (C) between the injector pump and the injectors
    (D) between the injector fuel return line and the fuel tank

14. The secondary filter is usually installed _____.   14. _____
    (A) between the fuel tank and the transfer pump
    (B) between the fuel transfer pump and the injector pump
    (C) between the injector pump and the injectors
    (D) between the injector fuel return line and the fuel tank

15. Dual filters can be configured in _____.   15. _____
    (A) series, where all fuel goes through the first and
        then the second filter
    (B) parallel, where a portion of the fuel passes through
        each filter
    (C) Either of the above.
    (D) Neither of the above.

16. When engines are exposed to extremely dusty   16. _____
    conditions, dual filters are usually arranged in _____.
    (A) series
    (B) parallel
    (C) a combination of series and parallel
    (D) None of the above.

17. Which of the following dual-filter arrangements can   17. _____
    move the largest volume of fuel thought the system
    at the fastest rate?
    (A) series
    (B) parallel
    (C) a combination of series and parallel
    (D) None of the above.

18. The first stage of a three-stage filtration system removes   18. _____
    contaminants as small as 25–30 microns and is known
    as _____.
    (A) separation
    (B) coalescing
    (C) simple filtration
    (D) centrifugal filtration

Name _____

19. The second stage of a three-stage filtration system removes lightweight droplets as small as 10–15 microns and is known as _____.
    (A) separation
    (B) coalescing
    (C) simple filtration
    (D) centrifugal filtration

19. _____

20. The third stage of a three-stage filtration system removes any remaining contaminants and is known as _____.
    (A) separation
    (B) coalescing
    (C) simple filtration
    (D) centrifugal filtration

20. _____

21. When using a dual-filter arrangement that utilizes a primary and secondary filter, which filter should typically be changed more often?
    (A) Primary.
    (B) Secondary.
    (C) Both should always be changed at the same time.
    (D) Filters should only be cleaned, not changed.

21. _____

Servicing Filters

22. The wiring harness, starting motor, and other electrical equipment must be shielded during fuel filter maintenance because diesel fuel _____.
    (A) could start a fire
    (B) will leave sticky deposits that attract dirt
    (C) can permanently damage electrical insulation
    (D) will short out electrical connections

22. _____

23. Care must be taken to avoid overtightening filters during installation because overtightening could cause _____.
    (A) the threads to be distorted
    (B) the filter element's seal to be damaged
    (C) Either of the above.
    (D) Neither of the above.

23. _____

24. The primary purpose of bleeding a fuel line is to _____.
    (A) remove any water from the line
    (B) replace old, contaminated fuel with new fuel
    (C) completely evacuate all fuel from a line
    (D) remove any entrapped air from the line

24. _____

25. When air enters the fuel system through leaks or turbulence and does not vent completely at the tank, air collection will occur in the _____.
    (A) fuel filter
    (B) fuel tank
    (C) fuel filler
    (D) fuel valve

25. _____

26. Soft throttle is a condition that refers to _____.
    (A) hypersensitivity of the engine to accelerator pressure
    (B) inability of an engine to return to idle speed when accelerator is released
    (C) insufficient spring-return tension on accelerator pedal
    (D) lack of response to accelerator pressure as a result of excess air in filters

26. _____

27. Technician A says that one hour of idling will cause as much diesel engine wear as 150 miles of driving. Technician B says that an engine that is allowed to idle will cool down faster than an engine that is shut down immediately after use. Who is correct?
    (A) A only.
    (B) B only.
    (C) C Both A & B.
    (D) Neither A nor B.

27. _____

28. To improve cold engine performance and reduce wear when temperatures are low enough to cause wax crystal formation in diesel fuel, fuel is usually kept warm by _____.
    (A) extended idling of the engine to keep it warm
    (B) parking the truck in a heated building
    (C) filling the tanks just prior to departure
    (D) use of a fuel heater

28. _____

Name _____

29. In some stationary and marine diesel installations, fuel leaving the engine is cooled before it returns to the fuel tank by _____.

    (A) circulation through a refrigerant system

    (B) circulation through a large air-cooled radiator

    (C) formation of wax crystals in the fuel

    (D) use of a raw-water fuel cooler

29. _____

30. Excessive fuel temperatures (above 90°F) can cause _____.

    (A) a brake horsepower loss

    (B) excessive waxing of fuel

    (C) higher than normal combustion temperatures

    (D) overheating of the turbine side of the turbo

30. _____

Name _____

Date _____

Instructor _____

Score _____ Text pages 349–368

Chapter 17

Injection System Fundamentals

After studying this chapter and completing supplemental exercises, you will be able to:

- List the five types of fuel injection systems commonly used today and classify each as either a high pressure or low pressure system.
- Define and explain the importance of metering, timing, rate control, atomization, injection start and cut-off, and proper pressurization to the fuel injection system.
- Name the major components of the port and helix metering system and describe its operation.
- Name the major components of a sleeve metering system and describe its operation.
- Name the major components of an inlet metering system and describe its operation.
- Name the three major factors that are used to control fuel delivery in P-T fuel injection systems, and describe the system's basic operating principles.
- Describe the operation of unit injection systems.
- List six reasons why a governor is needed on a diesel engine.
- Understand the terminology of governors.

Diesel Fuel Injection Systems

1. Distributor pumps are best suited for _____.

    (A) stationary engines

    (B) larger diesel engines

    (C) single-cylinder diesel applications

    (D) light and medium duty car and truck diesel engines

1. _____

For questions 2–8, match the following diesel fuel injection system types with their descriptions.

(A) Individual jerk pump

(B) Multiple-plunger inline pump

(C) Unit injector

(D) Pressure-time injection

(E) Distributor pump injection

(F) Hydraulic electronic unit injector

(G) Common rail injection

2. Uses electrically operated injectors to discharge fuel into the system from a high-pressure fuel rail.

2. _____

3. Uses a spinning rotor to distribute pressurized fuel to the individual injectors in the proper cylinder firing sequence.

3. _____

4. Times and meters the fuel and uses high pressure engine oil to pressurize and atomize fuel charge.

4. _____

5. Controls fuel metering by engine speed and fuel pressure.

5. _____

6. Times, atomizes, meters, and pressurizes the fuel within the injector body or unit serving each cylinder.

6. _____

7. Contained in its own housing and serving a single cylinder.

7. _____

8. Uses a number of individual jerk pumps contained in one common housing.

8. _____

9. Low pressure injection systems such as unit injectors and pressure-time systems can have supply pressures as low as _____.

9. _____

(A) 3–5 psi

(B) 50–75 psi

(C) 2000–3000 psi

(D) 20,000–30,000 psi

Name _____

Diesel Fuel Injection System Tasks

For questions 10–14, match the following terms with the descriptions.

   (A) atomizing
   (B) timing
   (C) fuel metering
   (D) fuel penetration
   (E) rate control

10. A fuel system's ability to deliver the same quantity of fuel to each cylinder for every power stroke of the engine at a given rpm is called _____.

   10. _____

11. A fuel system's ability to inject fuel at the proper point in the combustion cycle is called _____.

   11. _____

12. The breaking up of injected fuel into small particles that form a mist-like spray as it enters the cylinder is called _____.

   12. _____

13. A fuel system's ability to inject fuel in a manner that manages combustion and the degree of pressure rise in the cylinder is called _____.

   13. _____

14. The distance the fuel particles travel using their own kinetic energy as they leave the injector or nozzle is termed _____.

   14. _____

Fuel Metering

15. When servicing port and helix metering systems, plunger and barrel assemblies should always be replaced _____.

   15. _____

   (A) whenever the unit is serviced
   (B) on a regular scheduled maintenance interval
   (C) only as an assembly
   (D) only if both parts are damaged or excessively worn

16. In a port and helix system, the plunger moves up and down inside the barrel, opening and closing the ports in the barrel which in turn _____.

   16. _____

   (A) controls fuel flow inside and pressure inside the unit
   (B) controls the start and end of the injection period
   (C) Both of the above.
   (D) Neither of the above.

17. In a port and helix system, the point in the injection cycle that is the actual start of injection is known as _____.

    (A) combustion

    (B) port opening

    (C) port closing

    (D) poststroke

17. _____

For questions 18–21, match the following proper phase of the plunger stroke with its description.

    (A) prestroke

    (B) retractive stroke

    (C) effective stroke

    (D) residual stroke

18. The travel of the plunger from the end of prestroke to the opening of the delivery valve is known as _____.

18. _____

19. The travel of the pump plunger from the end of the retractive stroke to the opening of the spill port by the helix of the pump plunger is known as the _____.

19. _____

20. The travel between the end of the effective stroke and the top dead center position of the plunger is known as the _____.

20. _____

21. The travel of the pump plunger from its bottom dead center position to the start of delivery is known as the _____.

21. _____

22. The pulling back of a small amount of fuel in the injection line to close the nozzle quickly is known as _____.

    (A) injection line prestroke

    (B) injection line retraction

    (C) effective delivery

    (D) injection line residualization

22. _____

23. As fuel is trapped above the plunger and the delivery valve is forced off its seat, fuel flows around it and the valve remains open until fuel flow stops, which occurs when _____.

    (A) the nozzle valve unseats

    (B) combustion occurs

    (C) the port is covered by the helix

    (D) the port is uncovered by the helix

23. _____

Name _____

24. After lowered line pressure allows the injection nozzle to seat and stop fuel delivery to the combustion chamber, the delivery valve maintains a certain amount of line pressure so that _____.
    (A) the nozzle doesn't dribble
    (B) the timing will be retarded
    (C) succeeding injection cycles do not have to fill the line with fuel
    (D) delivery and retraction can all happen slowly

24. _____

25. A(n) _____ reduces the wear on the high pressure fuel system caused by the fast flowing diesel fuel and prevents pressure waves from damaging the pumping element.
    (A) starting groove
    (B) return flow restrictor
    (C) plunger
    (D) governor

25. _____

26. A diesel engine will start more quickly when fuel injection is _____ during the cranking process.
    (A) retarded
    (B) advanced
    (C) static
    (D) oscillating

26. _____

27. Since the plungers of inline pumps have a constant stroke, the method used to change the quantity of fuel delivered each stroke is using the _____.
    (A) helix and vertical groove cuts on the plunger
    (B) tapered sleeve plunger
    (C) variable-tilt swash plate
    (D) throttle-actuator valve

27. _____

28. The injection system that uses a sliding collar through which the stroking plunger moves is the _____.
    (A) sleeve metering system
    (B) inlet metering system
    (C) pressure-time metering system
    (D) unit injector metering system

28. _____

29. On a sleeve metering type system, fuel cannot go through the fuel outlet during the plunger's downward stroke because it is blocked by the _____.

    (A) governor

    (B) cam lobe

    (C) delivery valve

    (D) control sleeve

29. _____

For questions 30–32, match the following proper metering system with its description.

    (A) sleeve metering system

    (B) inlet metering system

    (C) pressure-time metering system

    (D) unit injector metering system

30. The type of system developed by Vernon Roosa that measures the fuel charge before it reaches the main pumping element is the _____.

30. _____

31. The type of fuel system that meters fuel based on orifice opening of the injector, how long the orifice is open, and the pressure supplied to the injector is the _____.

31. _____

32. The type of system where low pressure fuel from the fuel pump is delivered to the inlet fuel manifold and depends upon the rocker arm motion as well as the rotation of the plunger inside its barrel to meter and pressurize the fuel charge is known as the _____.

32. _____

33. On a unit injection system, each injector's fuel control rack is connected to a control tube that is in turn actuated by the _____.

    (A) fuel pump

    (B) injector pump

    (C) governor

    (D) transfer pump

33. _____

Name _____

Governing Engine Speed

34. A diesel engine's rotational speed is controlled by _____.

    (A) varying the amount of air introduced into the cylinders

    (B) varying the amount of fuel introduced into the cylinders

    (C) varying the diesel fuel grades introduced into the cylinder

    (D) None of the above.

34. _____

35. The governor or fuel control system on a diesel engine must perform the following actions for proper operation *except*:

    (A) furnish additional fuel when the engine lugs to maximum torque.

    (B) stall the engine after idling for a set amount of time.

    (C) limit the maximum engine speed.

    (D) provide sufficient fuel for starting the engine.

35. _____

For questions 36–39, match each type of engine speed governing to its description.

    (A) Limiting speed governor

    (B) Variable speed governor

    (C) Constant speed governor

    (D) Overspeed governor

36. The type of governor that maintains engine speed at a steady rpm regardless of load.

36. _____

37. The type of governor that prevents the engine from exceeding a specified maximum speed.

37. _____

38. The type of governor that controls low idle speed and high idle speed but allows the operator to control all speeds between low and high idle.

38. _____

39. The type of governor that gives the engine automatic speed control and is easily adjusted during operation.

39. _____

For questions 40–43, match each speed to its description.

    (A) high idle speed

    (B) low idle speed

    (C) rated speed

    (D) maximum torque speed

40. The highest rpm that the governor permits the engine to operate is called the _____.

40. _____

41. The rpm at which the engine generates the most torque is called the _____.

41. _____

42. The lowest rpm at which the governor will permit the engine to run is called the _____.

42. _____

43. The engine rpm at which the engine will generate its maximum horsepower is called the _____.

43. _____

44. The change in engine speed caused by a change in engine load is called _____.

    (A) speed droop

    (B) under run

    (C) over run

    (D) deadband

44. _____

45. A condition where the governor fails to maintain low idle speed whenever the engine rpms drop quickly from higher speeds is called _____.

    (A) speed droop

    (B) under run

    (C) over run

    (D) deadband

45. _____

46. A narrow speed range during which no measurable speed correction is made by the governor is called _____.

    (A) speed droop

    (B) under run

    (C) over run

    (D) deadband

46. _____

47. Define *sensitivity* as used in this chapter.

_____

_____

_____

Name _____

48. Define *promptness* as used in this chapter.

_____

_____

_____

49. Continuous engine speed fluctuation (slowing down and speeding up) from the desired rpm setting is called _____.

    (A) sensitivity

    (B) promptness

    (C) hunting or surging

    (D) stability

49. _____

50. The ability of a governor to maintain the desired engine speed without fluctuations is called _____.

    (A) sensitivity

    (B) promptness

    (C) hunting or surging

    (D) stability

50. _____

51. The oldest and most universally used diesel engine governor is the _____ -type governor.

    (A) mechanical

    (B) hydraulic

    (C) servo

    (D) pneumatic

51. _____

52. As the flyweights on a mechanical governor move outward in response to speed increase, what action do they have on the fuel supplied to the cylinders?

    (A) Increase the fuel amount supplied.

    (B) Decrease the fuel amount supplied.

    (C) Maintain (neither increase nor decrease) the amount of fuel supplied.

    (D) No effect on the amount of fuel supplied.

52. _____

53. Subdivide all engine speed governing systems into their three separate functions.

_____

_____

_____

54. In an electronic governing diesel fuel injection system, the system controller performs all of the following actions *except*:

    (A) rectifies the ac signal from a sensor to dc current.

    (B) generates an appropriate output signal to an actuator.

    (C) controls the transmission shift points.

    (D) processes sensor inputs and compares against programmed specifications.

54. _____

55. The relationship, or error, between the change in fuel and the speed response by the engine is termed _____.

    (A) loss

    (B) gain

    (C) linear

    (D) nonlinear

55. _____

56. A small increase in fuel that results in a large speed increase would be an example of _____.

    (A) low loss

    (B) high loss

    (C) low gain

    (D) high gain

56. _____

57. A large increase in fuel that results in only a small increase in engine speed is known as _____.

    (A) low loss

    (B) high loss

    (C) low gain

    (D) high gain

57. _____

58. The type of governor that can react accordingly to intermittent low gain conditions through proportional control is called a(n) _____ governor.

    (A) gain

    (B) droop

    (C) stability

    (D) variable

58. _____

Name _____

59. When a stability function is added to electronic governing systems to provide corrections proportional not only to the amount of speed error, but also to the time the error is present, this type of governing is called _____.

    (A) isochronous governing

    (B) reactive governing

    (C) compensational governing

    (D) None of the above.

59. _____

60. On engines with large actuators, response to rapid speed deviations can be slow enough to cause speed overshoots. To correct for this, a setting that results in a reduction of transient speed error during sudden load changes is called _____.

    (A) real time compensation

    (B) on-line compensation

    (C) live-time compensation

    (D) dead time compensation

60. _____

Name _____

Date_____

Instructor_____

Score_____ Text pages 369–386

Chapter 18

Injection Nozzles

After studying this chapter and completing supplemental exercises, you will be able to:

- Give the location, name the major parts, and explain the operation of an injection nozzle holder.
- Describe the difference between open and closed nozzle designs.
- Describe the construction and operation of hole, pintle, and Pentaux® nozzles.
- Explain how spray hole design, opening pressure, differential ratio, needle and spindle mass, valve guide diameter, needle lift, fuel sac design, and diameter affect hole nozzle operation and performance.
- Successfully remove and install a nozzle holder and nozzle.
- Successfully disassemble, inspect, clean, reassemble, and test nozzle holders and nozzles.
- Describe the operation and service procedures for pencil injection nozzles.
- Describe the types of fuel injection tubing and connections used for high pressure injection fuel lines.

Nozzle Holders

1. All injector nozzles are enclosed in nozzle holders that are mounted in the _____.

    (A) injector pump

    (B) cylinder head

    (C) cylinder block

    (D) cylinder liner

1. _____

2. All of the following are functions of nozzle holders, *except*:
   (A) they provide a mechanism for piston cooling.
   (B) they position the nozzle in the engine cylinder.
   (C) they hold the needed spring and pressure adjustments.
   (D) they provide a means for conducting fuel to the nozzle and combustion chamber.

2. _____

3. The nozzle spacer contains two locating pins that position the nozzle radially to ensure _____.
   (A) proper alignment of the delivery pipe
   (B) the injector does not turn in the bore
   (C) proper spray pattern orientation to the combustion chamber
   (D) proper heat transfer from the combustion chamber

3. _____

4. The slight amount of fuel leakage that occurs past the nozzle valve's major outside diameter _____.
   (A) should be minimized to avoid crankcase dilution
   (B) should be precluded by proper torquing of the cap nut
   (C) can cause heavy black exhaust smoke
   (D) is used to lubricate the valve seat and adjusting spring

4. _____

5. Which type of injection nozzles has no valve to stop the flow of fuel from the nozzle tip?
   (A) Open injector nozzles.
   (B) Closed injector nozzles.
   (C) Pintle injector nozzles.
   (D) Hole nozzles.

5. _____

6. Technician A says that open injector nozzles have a spring-loaded valve located near the nozzle's exit orifice. Technician B says that delay injector nozzles have a spring-loaded valve located near the nozzle's exit orifice. Who is correct?
   (A) A only.
   (B) B only.
   (C) Both A & B.
   (D) Neither A nor B.

6. _____

Name _____

7. Technician A says that open injector nozzles are prone to fuel leakage, or "dribble," through the tip. Technician B says that open injector nozzles clog easily. Who is correct?

(A) A only.

(B) B only.

(C) Both A & B.

(D) Neither A nor B.

7. _____

8. Direct injection, open combustion chamber diesel engines, such as those used in heavy-duty truck applications, mainly use _____.

(A) short-stem open injector nozzles

(B) long-stem hole injector nozzles

(C) large-diameter stem injector nozzles

(D) None of the above.

8. _____

9. The type of injector nozzle that requires less mounting space between cylinder head valves is _____.

(A) short-stem hole injector nozzles

(B) long-stem hole injector nozzles

(C) large-diameter stem injector nozzles

(D) None of the above.

9. _____

10. The number, diameter, and position of _____ determine how well the fuel entering the combustion chamber is atomized.

(A) injector lines

(B) nozzle holders

(C) pump delivery heads

(D) spray holes

10. _____

11. The ratio between the diameter of the valve guide and the seat is referred to as the _____.

(A) guide ratio

(B) seat ratio

(C) differential ratio

(D) annulus ratio

11. _____

12. Technician A says that a large differential ratio decreases the amount of stroke-to-stroke variation between injectors. Technician B says that as the mass of the valve needle increases, the speed at which the needle moves also increases. Who is correct?

(A) A only.

(B) B only.

(C) Both A & B.

(D) Neither A nor B.

12. _____

13. A nozzle that is experiencing gas blowback of combustion gases through the nozzle opening _____.

(A) will make a chattering sound

(B) will cause excessive black smoking

(C) will have a very short seat life

(D) will have excessive carbon formation

13. _____

14. Too much valve needle lift will cause _____.

(A) excessive fuel flow

(B) excessive pressure drop

(C) Both of the above.

(D) Neither of the above.

14. _____

15. There is a direct relationship between the fuel sac volume under the seat and the _____.

(A) level of hydrocarbon emissions

(B) amount of turbo boost required

(C) pressure needed to seat the valve quickly

(D) diameter of the valve needle

15. _____

16. Pintle injector nozzles are typically used in _____.

(A) open combustion chamber heavy-duty truck engines

(B) single-cylinder stationary engines

(C) large-bore, slow-speed engines

(D) small-bore, high-speed engines

16. _____

17. To help reduce preignition and knocking, certain types of pintle nozzles that reduce the amount of fuel injected in the early stages of injection are used. These types of nozzles are classified as _____.

(A) advance nozzles

(B) delay nozzles

(C) emission nozzles

(D) annular nozzles

17. _____

Name _____

18. The "pilot" effect of a nozzle is more effective _____.   18. _____

    (A) at idling when the valve lift is low

    (B) at high speeds when the valve lift is low

    (C) at idling when the valve lift is high

    (D) at high speeds when the valve lift is high

19. The CAV Pentaux® nozzle is designed with an auxiliary   19. _____
spray hole to _____.

    (A) prevent engine "run-on" when the engine is stopped

    (B) prevent injector dribble at low or idle speeds

    (C) relieve blowback from combustion pressures

    (D) assist in easy starting in cold weather conditions

Servicing Fuel Injector Holders and Nozzles

20. If, during servicing of a fuel injector nozzle, a   20. _____
technician were to inadvertently increase the injector
opening pressure, which symptom could occur?

    (A) There would be a marked decrease in the delay time.

    (B) The engine would operate with decreased
emissions and fuel consumption.

    (C) Both of the above.

    (D) Neither of the above.

21. One of the factors that can severely reduce the service   21. _____
life of fuel injectors is corrosion. A source of this
corrosion could be _____.

    (A) water in the fuel

    (B) sulfur in the fuel

    (C) Both of the above.

    (D) Neither of the above.

22. Loosening or cracking open the individual fuel injector   22. _____
lines at the injector, one at a time, while listening for
changes in the engine idle will identify a faulty or
nonfiring injector, because when loosened, a faulty
injector will cause engine idle to _____.

    (A) speed up

    (B) slow down

    (C) remain unchanged

    (D) surge

23. The most important factor to remember when servicing fuel injection systems is _____.
    (A) the type of fuel being used
    (B) how long the system will be open
    (C) using the right tools to disconnect lines
    (D) cleanliness

23. _____

24. What is the major danger to be avoided when checking the high-pressure spray pattern of an injector when using a test stand?
    (A) Contaminating the injector.
    (B) Injuring personnel with high-pressure spray puncturing human skin.
    (C) Setting test pressure incorrectly.
    (D) Damaging the test stand.

24. _____

25. The exterior surface of the injector nozzle should be cleaned by _____.
    (A) brushing with a fine-wire brass brush
    (B) using a stiff steel-wire brush on a bench grinder
    (C) beadblasting the nozzle
    (D) polishing with a fine-grade crocus cloth

25. _____

Items 26 through 29. Match the following injector tests with their descriptions.

    (A) Valve seat test
    (B) Back leakage test
    (C) Spray pattern test
    (D) Chatter test

26. With an injector mounted on a test-bench tester, this test would indicate an acceptable nozzle based on only a slight wetting of the nozzle tip after five seconds.

26. _____

27. With an injector mounted on a test-bench tester, this test would indicate any problems with the nozzle fit in the bore or the lapped surfaces of the nozzle body and holder.

27. _____

28. With an injector mounted on a test-bench tester, this test would indicate an acceptable injector based on correct angularity and uniformity of the discharge when the hand pump is operated to simulate normal injector operation.

28. _____

Name _____

29. With an injector mounted on a test-bench tester (other than a CAV Pentaux® nozzle), this test would indicate a possible sticking injector valve because no sounds were heard from the injector during operation of the hand pump.

29. _____

30. For proper inspection of the nozzle to occur, the inspector should _____.
    (A) visually inspect the nozzle assembly without disassembling it
    (B) clean the nozzle holes with a soft brass brush
    (C) remove the nozzle cap nut prior to soaking in a carbon-removing cleaning agent
    (D) completely disassemble the nozzle holder and nozzle

30. _____

31. When cleaning injectors, the valves _____.
    (A) may be intermixed
    (B) should be replaced
    (C) should be kept with their original nozzle body
    (D) should be polished with an abrasive cloth

31. _____

32. When using jeweler's rouge and a lapping plate or block to clean a nozzle body, the nozzle should be lapped using what kind of motion?
    (A) Back and forth.
    (B) Circular.
    (C) Lapping only in one direction.
    (D) A figure eight pattern.

32. _____

33. When reassembling nozzles after cleaning, the lift height should be checked to be sure it is within specifications to avoid _____.
    (A) improper liftoff time
    (B) incorrect fuel flow
    (C) incorrect spray cone and pattern
    (D) All of the above.

33. _____

34. After reinstalling the nozzles in the engine, the nozzles should be bled by cranking the engine over with the fuel control in the _____ position.

    34. _____

    (A) fully closed
    (B) partially open
    (C) fully open
    (D) in the "stop" position

Pencil Nozzles

---

35. Pencil nozzles operate in the same way as the other nozzles covered in this chapter, *except*:

    35. _____

    (A) pencil injectors will not give off a chatter.
    (B) dribble is acceptable in pencil injectors.
    (C) its needle valve opens and closes more slowly.
    (D) its needle valve opens and closes more rapidly.

36. A capped pencil nozzle differs from a regular pencil nozzle in that _____.

    36. _____

    (A) it uses multiple fuel return lines
    (B) it uses a different input line
    (C) leak-off fuel does not accumulate in the nozzle cap
    (D) it does not use a return line

37. To properly clean a pencil nozzle, it is recommended that the nozzle _____.

    37. _____

    (A) be completely disassembled
    (B) not be disassembled
    (C) be completely submerged to remove the anti-rust coating on the nozzle body
    (D) not have its opening and fuel lines capped off

38. When testing a pencil nozzle for valve lift, the operator should be careful to _____.

    38. _____

    (A) bottom the valve with a hard positive pressure to properly seat the valve
    (B) avoid manually bottoming the valve to prevent bending
    (C) remove the lift screw first
    (D) unseat the lift screw by turning it clockwise until the valve begins to open

Name _____

39. When adjusting the lift, it should always be set _____.
    (A) before checking spray pattern and chatter
    (B) after checking spray pattern and chatter
    (C) after being installed in the engine
    (D) only by a certified technician

39. _____

40. Before reinstalling a pencil nozzle, _____.
    (A) clean the cylinder bore with a bore cleaning tool
    (B) clean and check the sealing surfaces of the cylinder head
    (C) Both of the above.
    (D) Neither of the above.

40. _____

Name _____

Date_____

Instructor_____

Score_____ Text pages 387–408

Chapter 19

Multiple Plunger Inline Injection Pumps

After studying this chapter and completing supplemental exercises, you will be able to:

* Name the major components in a multiple plunger inline pump fuel injection system.
* Name the components of a typical inline fuel injection pump and describe how they operate.
* Explain the function and operation of a typical inline injection pump automatic timing device.
* Properly remove and install an inline fuel injection pump.
* Describe the three methods used to time an inline injection pump.
* Properly bleed all air from the fuel lines.
* Perform diagnostic tests to check for proper pump operating pressures, relief valve operation, and fuel line restrictions.
* Describe the various devices used on injection pumps to control the generation of black exhaust smoke during acceleration.

Inline Injection Pumps

1. Although a number of companies manufacture multiple plunger inline injection pumps, the majority are manufactured by _____.

    (A) Robert Bosch Corporation

    (B) AMBAC International

    (C) Lucas CAV

    (D) Caterpillar, Inc.

1. _____

191

Inline Injection Pump Components

2. On an inline injection pump, each injection nozzle is _____.
   (A) operated by rocker arm actuation
   (B) equipped with its own fuel return line
   (C) located within the pump
   (D) operated by a separate pump

2. _____

3. How many plunger and barrel assemblies exist for each cylinder of an inline pump?
   (A) One.
   (B) Two.
   (C) Four.
   (D) Six.

3. _____

4. Provided the injection pump is properly installed and timed, injection position is synchronized with the proper crankshaft position using a torsion-proof _____.
   (A) roller tappet
   (B) clutch disk
   (C) chain drive
   (D) coupling element

4. _____

5. An inline injector pump's plungers are driven by the pump's _____.
   (A) idler gear
   (B) clutch disk
   (C) camshaft
   (D) barrel

5. _____

6. In a four-stroke engine, the speed of the injection pump camshaft is the same as the speed of the engine's _____.
   (A) crankshaft
   (B) camshaft
   (C) Both of the above.
   (D) Neither of the above.

6. _____

Name _____

7. The delivery line is sealed from the barrel during the
   intake stroke by the _____.
   (A) plunger return spring
   (B) control rod
   (C) control rack
   (D) delivery valve

7. _____

8. To prevent nozzle dribble, pressure in the injection line
   is relieved by the _____.
   (A) control rod
   (B) control rack
   (C) delivery valve
   (D) plunger return spring

8. _____

9. Governor action is transmitted to the pumping plunger
   by the _____.
   (A) plunger return spring
   (B) control rod
   (C) control rack
   (D) delivery valve

9. _____

10. Each plunger is moved up and down inside the barrel
    housing by the action of the _____.
    (A) injection pump camshaft
    (B) control rod
    (C) control rack
    (D) delivery valve

10. _____

11. For injection to begin, the pumping plunger must
    be lifted until it closes off the inlet fuel ports. This is
    known as _____.
    (A) nozzle dribble
    (B) lift-to-port closure
    (C) bottom dead center
    (D) helix closure

11. _____

12. Identify the four principle plunger positions of one complete injection cycle.

(A) _____ (C) _____

(B) _____ (D) _____

A   B   C   D

13. Name two ways inline injection pumps can be classified.

_____

_____

14. Although engine speed may increase or decrease, the burn time for diesel fuel will remain basically the same. To account for the changing speeds, the point of injection is adjusted by _____.

    14. _____

(A) a vacuum advance unit

(B) an automatic timing advance unit

(C) advancing the static timing when installing the pump

(D) None of the above.

15. Timing devices that are lubricated from the engine's pressurized oil system are classified as _____.

    15. _____

(A) open timing devices

(B) closed timing devices

(C) Either of the above.

(D) Neither of the above.

16. Timing devices that are filled with a lubricant at the time of manufacture and do not require servicing during their normal service life are called _____.

    16. _____

(A) open timing devices

(B) closed timing devices

(C) Either of the above.

(D) Neither of the above.

Name _____

Inline Pump Testing and Service

17. Before removing an inline injection pump, the operator should first _____.
    - (A) mark the timing point on the front fan
    - (B) align the timing marks on the rocker arms
    - (C) remove the flywheel
    - (D) align the timing marks with #1 cylinder on TDC

17. _____

18. The best way to confirm that a cylinder is on its compression stroke is to _____.
    - (A) look at the timing mark on the flywheel
    - (B) look at the timing mark on the front damper
    - (C) check for lash in both intake and exhaust valves
    - (D) check pulley timing marks

18. _____

19. If a technician aligned the timing marks but one of the valves for the cylinder was open, the technician should _____.
    - (A) proceed
    - (B) adjust the valve
    - (C) turn the engine enough to rotate the crankshaft 360°
    - (D) turn the engine enough to rotate the camshaft 360°

19. _____

20. After removal and prior to installation, the technician should take care _____.
    - (A) to keep the engine at room temperature
    - (B) to keep the pump at room temperature
    - (C) to not turn the crankshaft
    - (D) None of the above.

20. _____

21. When reinstalling an injector pump, a new O-ring or gasket should be installed on the pump mounting flange _____.
    - (A) only if the old one was damaged or leaking
    - (B) only if the old one was missing or incorrect
    - (C) any time the pump has been removed
    - (D) None of the above.

21. _____

22. During reinstallation, a static spill timing check should be done to check pump-to-engine timing. The term *static* is used because _____.

    (A) the pump will not be moved

    (B) of disruption of the electrical field

    (C) the test is done while the engine is not running

    (D) the test is done before the pump is mounted to the engine

22. _____

23. What are the three methods that can be used to set spill timing?

    _____

    _____

    _____

24. Of the three test methods used to set spill timing, which is the simplest and most accurate method of setting the injection pump to engine timing?

    _____

25. Which method of spill timing requires a test stand?

    _____

26. Which method of spill timing is the least preferable and should only be used when neither of the other two methods is available?

    _____

Basic Troubleshooting

27. When performing basic troubleshooting, low power, rough running, or stalling could indicate that _____.

    (A) too much fuel is reaching the injection pump

    (B) not enough fuel is reaching the injection pump

    (C) too much air is entrapped in the injector pump

    (D) not enough air is entrapped in the injector pump

27. _____

28. To check the pressure relief valve, the technician should disconnect the fuel line that leads from the _____.

    (A) tank to the primary filter

    (B) primary filter to the transfer pump

    (C) transfer pump to the secondary filter

    (D) secondary filter to the injector pump

28. _____

Name _____

29. A transfer pump restriction check should be made
using a(n) _____.

29. _____

(A) vacuum gauge

(B) manometer tube

(C) Either of the above.

(D) Neither of the above.

Acceleration Smoke Controls

30. The problem of diesel engine acceleration causing
excess black smoke is greater in which type of engines?

30. _____

(A) Naturally aspirated.

(B) Turbocharged.

(C) Both of the above.

(D) Neither of the above.

31. An aneroid/boost compensator is a pollution control
device that helps to reduce black smoke caused by

_____.

31. _____

(A) overfueling and air lag time

(B) injector dribbling

(C) exhaust restrictions

(D) intake air restrictions

32. During startup, the aneroid is disconnected from the
control rack by _____.

32. _____

(A) the operator

(B) vacuum pressure

(C) a hydraulic activator

(D) electric controls

33. An external pneumatic pollution control device that
acts directly on the fuel rack but independently of the
governor is the _____.

33. _____

(A) smoke diaphragm

(B) puff limiter

(C) exhaust gas recirculator

(D) aneroid

34. The type of acceleration smoke control device used to
    prevent overfueling during acceleration on unit
    injection-type diesels such as Detroit Diesel engines
    is a(n) _____.
    (A) puff limiter
    (B) aneroid
    (C) pneumatic activator
    (D) throttle-delay mechanism

34. _____

35. Altitude-pressure compensators are typically used on
    only what type of diesel engines?
    (A) Naturally aspirated.
    (B) Turbocharged.
    (C) Both of the above.
    (D) Neither of the above.

35. _____

Name _____

Date_____

Instructor_____

Score_____Text pages 409–424

Chapter 20
Distributor Injection Pumps

After studying this chapter and completing supplemental exercises, you will be able to:

- Explain the major difference between multiple plunger inline injection pumps and distributor injection pumps.
- Describe the operating principles and major components of the single-plunger distributor injection pump.
- Describe the operating principles and major components of opposed plunger, inlet metered distributor injection pumps.
- Properly remove, install, and calibrate distributor injection pumps.

Distributor Injection Pumps

1. A distributor injection pump uses _____ to meter and deliver pressurized fuel to the fuel injectors at all cylinders.

    (A) one pumping element per cylinder

    (B) dual pumping elements

    (C) a single pumping element

    (D) None of the above.

1. _____

2. Distributor pumps are compact injection pumps designed for applications with _____ speed requirements, such as medium to heavy-duty trucks, farm equipment, and tractors.

    (A) relatively broad

    (B) relatively narrow

    (C) generally high

    (D) generally low

2. _____

3. Name two differences in distributor pump designs between manufacturers.

_____

_____

Single-Plunger Distributor Injection Pumps

4. On an AMBAC Model 100 single-plunger distributor pump, the plunger assembly rides on a(n) _____ _____ to produce the reciprocating movement needed to pressurize the fuel.

4. _____

5. The plunger is also rotated by the camshaft by a(n) _____ _____ to distribute the fuel to the outlet ducts.

5. _____

6. The transfer fuel pump is driven by the _____.

    (A) engine camshaft

    (B) governor driveshaft

    (C) distributor pump driveshaft

    (D) engine idler gear

6. _____

7. The hydraulic head of a single-plunger distributor pump is a complete assembly that mounts to the pump _____.

7. _____

8. List the main components of the hydraulic head of a single-plunger distributor pump.

_____

_____

_____

_____

_____

_____

_____

Name _____

9. On an AMBAC Model 100 single-plunger distributor pump, the plunger fits into the central bore of the _____ _____.

9. _____

10. The upper end of the central bore is counterbored and threaded to receive the _____ _____.

10. _____

11. An AMBAC Model 100 single-plunger distributor injection pump is being discussed. Technician A says that the plunger makes one complete revolution for every revolution of the camshaft. Technician B says that the plunger is lapped and mated to the head and metering sleeve so these components must be serviced as a unit. Who is right?

11. _____

   (A) A only.

   (B) B only.

   (C) Both A & B.

   (D) Neither A nor B.

12. As it moves vertically through the pumping cycle, the plunger _____ continuously.

12. _____

13. On an eight-cylinder engine, a four lobe cam actuates the plunger _____ times for every two revolutions of the pump camshaft.

13. _____

14. The single-plunger distributor pump is lubricated using _____.

14. _____

   (A) diesel fuel

   (B) engine coolant

   (C) engine oil

   (D) its own oil sump

15. Fuel enters the pump's sump and head cavity while the plunger is at the _____ of its stroke.

15. _____

16. The rotary and vertical movement of the plunger are so placed in relation to the outlet ports that the vertical distributing slot overlaps _____ outlet duct(s) during the effective portion of each stroke.

16. _____

   (A) one

   (B) two

   (C) four

   (D) eight

17. The _____ _____ position in relation to the fixed port closing position controls the amount of fuel delivered per stoke.

17. _____

18. At the _____-_____ position, the metering sleeve is at the bottom of its travel.

18. _____

19. The distance the plunger moves from the moment of port closing until the metering port is uncovered and the pressure is relieved is called the _____ _____.

19. _____

20. Name two functions of the single-plunger distributor pump delivery valve.

_____

_____

21. The single-plunger distributor pump's _____ controls fuel delivery by varying the position of the metering sleeve in the hydraulic head, thus maintaining a specified minimum and maximum rpm and providing torque control throughout the engine's operating range.

(A) transfer pump

(B) governor

(C) hydraulic head

(D) distributor

21. _____

22. The governor flyweights are turned at _____ speed.

(A) one-half engine

(B) one-fourth engine

(C) engine

(D) two times engine

22. _____

23. At peak torque, maximum fuel delivery is attained when the _____ contacts the stop plate.

(A) droop screw

(B) fulcrum arm

(C) control rack

(D) stop screw

23. _____

24. The _____ responds to intake manifold pressures to limit fuel flow until enough air is present for complete combustion, thus eliminating the characteristic puff of black exhaust smoke during engine acceleration.

24. _____

25. The _____ _____ is the main driveshaft of the AMBAC Model 100 pump.

25. _____

Name _____

26. The Intravance camshaft contains _____ that move
the plunger up and down plus the gear that drives the
governor and rotates the plunger.
(A) springs
(B) lobes
(C) offsets
(D) gears

26. _____

27. The Intravance camshaft automatically varies the _____
of the fuel injection to match specific engine speeds.
(A) quantity
(B) timing
(C) atomization
(D) None of the above.

27. _____

28. The Intravance camshaft is capable of supplying _____
timing advance range(s).
(A) one
(B) two
(C) four
(D) infinite

28. _____

29. The splined sleeve of the Intravance camshaft is moved
by _____.
(A) air pressure
(B) oil pressure
(C) electronic solenoids
(D) spring pressure

29. _____

Opposed Plunger Inlet Metered Pumps

30. An opposed plunger inlet metered pump uses one
metering valve to meter the fuel and _____ opposed
plunger(s) to pump the fuel.
(A) one
(B) two or four
(C) six or eight
(D) None of the above.

30. _____

31. The _____ _____ on an opposed plunger distributor pump is used to distribute the metered fuel out through the hydraulic head to the cylinder injectors.

31. _____

32. Opposed plunger distributor pumps have a fuel delivery capacity of engines rated between _____ per cylinder.
    (A) 10–20 hp
    (B) 10–40 hp
    (C) 40–60 hp
    (D) 60–80 hp

32. _____

33. Name the major components of the Lucas CAV Model DPA inlet metered opposed plunger pump in the illustration shown.
    (A) _____   (D) _____
    (B) _____   (E) _____
    (C) _____

34. An opposed plunger distributor pump is lubricated by _____.
    (A) engine oil
    (B) diesel fuel
    (C) engine coolant
    (D) None of the above.

34. _____

35. A Lucas CAV Model DPA inlet metered opposed plunger distributor pump is driven by the driveshaft that couples the _____ to a drive hub located in the end of the pump housing.

35. _____

Name _____

36. The plungers on a Stanadyne Model DB4 injection pump are actuated toward each other simultaneously by an internal _____ through rollers and shoes that are carried in slots at the drive end of the rotor.

    (A) camshaft

    (B) rotor

    (C) cam ring

    (D) splined sleeve

36. _____

37. The number of cam lobes normally equals the number of _____ _____.

37. _____

38. The distributor rotor on a Stanadyne Model DB4 injection pump incorporates two _____ and a single axial bore with one discharge port to serve all head outlets to the injection lines.

    (A) charging ports

    (B) hydraulic heads

    (C) metering valves

    (D) delivery valves

38. _____

39. On an opposed plunger inlet metered pump, the _____ _____ contains the bore in which the rotor revolves, the metering valve bore, the charging ports, and the head discharge fittings.

39. _____

40. The automatic speed advance is a(n) _____ mechanism that advances or retards the beginning of fuel delivery from the pump.

    (A) electronic

    (B) pneumatic

    (C) mechanical

    (D) hydraulic

40. _____

41. The hydraulic head of an opposed plunger distributor pump is machined with bores and passages that allow fuel to flow to and from specific points such as _____.

    (A) from the transfer pump to the metering valve

    (B) from the metering valve to the charging ports

    (C) from the discharging ports to the discharge fittings

    (D) All of the above.

41. _____

42. The _____ _____ is lap-fitted to this design of hydraulic head and the governor weight retainer assembly is fastened to its drive end.

42. _____

43. The plungers of an opposed plunger distributor pump
are fitted to the rotor and are pushed inward by the
_____ to pump the diesel fuel.

(A) cam lobes

(B) rollers and shoes

(C) delivery springs

(D) None of the above.

43. _____

44. _____ _____ mount on the rotor and limit the outward
travel of the rollers and shoes in this type of pump,
which control the maximum fuel delivery rate.

44. _____

45. The _____ contained in the hydraulic head of an
opposed distributor pump regulates the volume of fuel
entering the rotor under the control of the governor.

(A) delivery valve

(B) metering valve

(C) annulus

(D) distributor

45. _____

46. The radial position of the metering valve, controlled
by the governor, regulates the flow of fuel into the
charging _____, which holds the charging ports.

46. _____

47. Name the two functions of the pressure regulating valve on an opposed plunger inlet
metered distributor pump.

_____

_____

48. Name the two ways the transfer pump can be adjusted.

_____

_____

49. During the _____ cycle of injection, the angled inlet
passages in the rotor are in registry with the ports in
the charging annulus, but the rotor discharge port is
not in registry with a head outlet.

49. _____

50. On some distributor pumps, such as the Lucas CAV
Model DPA, individual _____ _____ are installed in the
hydraulic head outlet bolts for each cylinder.

50. _____

51. Name two functions of the delivery valve(s) on an opposed plunger inlet metered distributor
pump.

_____

_____

Name _____

52. The opposed plunger inlet metered pump design permits the use of a direct acting hydraulic _____ _____ powered by fuel pressure from the transfer pump.

52. _____

53. The advance mechanism advances or retards start of fuel delivery in response to changes in _____ _____.

53. _____

54. On a mechanical governor in an opposed plunger distributor pump, the flyweights transmit force through the thrust sleeve, causing the governor lever to pivot and rotate the _____ _____, which reduces or increases the amount of fuel fed to the pumping cylinder.

54. _____

55. Regardless of the engine speed, a mechanical _____ rotates the metering valve in this type of pump to the shutoff position when required.

    (A) gear

    (B) lever

    (C) shutoff bar

    (D) fulcrum

55. _____

56. The _____ _____ of a mechanical governor provides sensitive speed control within the idling speed range.

56. _____

57. With a mechanical governor, the engine would _____ if the load was suddenly removed from the engine.

    (A) slow down

    (B) speed up

    (C) stall

    (D) None of the above.

57. _____

58. On a hydraulic governor transfer pump, fuel pressure is always exerted onto the lower area of the _____ _____.

58. _____

59. As the metering valve of a hydraulic governor moves up and down, it varies the area of the _____ _____ _____, which controls the amount of fuel flowing to the pumping cylinder.

59. _____

60. Adjusting the high and low _____ _____ of a hydraulic governor is simply a matter of turning the adjustment screws clockwise or counterclockwise to increase or decrease the spring force.

60. _____

61. Name the two types of electrical shut-off devices that can be installed on an opposed plunger distributor pump.

_____

_____

Distributor Injection Pump Removal and Installation

62. Technician A says it is safe to steam clean or wash down the injection pump housing while the engine is operating. Technician B says that when removing the injection tubing nut from the pump, hold the discharge fitting with a wrench to prevent it from loosening from the hydraulic head. Who is right?

    (A) A only.

    (B) B only.

    (C) Both A & B.

    (D) Neither A nor B.

62. _____

63. When removing a distributor pump, Technician A says that disconnected fuel lines and pump nozzles should be capped. Technician B rotates the engine until the number one cylinder is at top dead center. Who is right?

    (A) A only.

    (B) B only.

    (C) Both A & B.

    (D) Neither A nor B.

63. _____

64. After installing a distributor pump, Technician A says the lines must be bled of air and primed with fuel. Technician B says do not open the filter bleed if a hand primer is located after the filter. Instead, close the bleed screw and hand prime until a quantity of fuel flows air-free at the pump inlet line. Who is right?

    (A) A only.

    (B) B only.

    (C) Both A & B.

    (D) Neither A nor B.

64. _____

65. List the five procedures that are performed to calibrate an AMBAC Model 100 single-plunger distributor injection pump.

_____

_____

_____

_____

_____

Name _____

For questions 66–70, an AMBAC Model 100 single-plunger distributor injection pump is being calibrated.

66. Lift-to-port closure is measured using a(n) _____ _____.   66. _____

67. The _____ _____ adjustment is made by moving the stop plate horizontally in the direction of increased or decreased fuel, with the cam nose firmly against the stop plate.   67. _____

68. The point where contact is being made by the cam nose on the stop plate but no force is being exerted in the stop plate is _____ _____ _____.   68. _____

69. The peak torque set point is normally _____ below rated speed.   69. _____
   (A) 100–200 rpm
   (B) 200–300 rpm
   (C) 300–400 rpm
   (D) 500–600 rpm

70. The droop screw set point is usually about _____ below the peak torque set point.   70. _____
   (A) 100 rpm
   (B) 200 rpm
   (C) 300 rpm
   (D) 400 rpm

Name _____

Date _____

Instructor _____

Score _____ Text pages 425–434

Chapter 21

Unit Injector Fuel Injection Systems

After studying this chapter and completing supplemental exercises, you will be able to:

- Describe the fuel flow routing in an engine equipped with unit injection.
- Name the four functions of the unit injector.
- Describe how the unit injector is mounted in the engine and how it is activated by rocker arm action.
- Explain the basic operating principles of electronic unit injectors.
- Describe the proper operation of hydraulic electronic unit injectors.
- Perform a fuel spill back check.
- Perform an engine tune-up on a unit injection system.
- List the basic design characteristics of the Detroit Diesel Series 60 engine.
- Perform valve clearance adjustment and injector timing adjustment on Detroit Diesel Series 60 engines.

Basics of Unit Injection

1. Name the two ways of controlling unit injector operation.

_____

_____

2. Unit injection is a low pressure fuel system, with fuel delivered to the unit injectors at pressures averaging between _____.

    (A) 15–30 psi

    (B) 30–45 psi

    (C) 50–75 psi

    (D) 70–90 psi

2. _____

3. To avoid confusion when the fuel lines are installed, the _____ _____ are identified by the words *in* and *out* cast or stamped on the side of the cylinder head.

3. _____

4. Once in the fuel manifold, fuel passes through jumper pipes into the inlet side of each _____ _____.

4. _____

5. What happens to the fuel that is not injected?

_____

6. The _____ _____ at the end of the return fuel manifold maintains the manifold pressure inside the cylinder head.

    (A) check valve

    (B) restrictor fitting

    (C) metering valve

    (D) stop cock

6. _____

7. Name the four main functions of a mechanical unit injector.

_____

_____

_____

_____

Name _____

8. List the components of a mechanical unit injector.

(A) _____   (N) _____

(B) _____   (O) _____

(C) _____   (P) _____

(D) _____   (Q) _____

(E) _____   (R) _____

(F) _____   (S) _____

(G) _____   (T) _____

(H) _____   (U) _____

(I) _____   (V) _____

(J) _____   (W) _____

(K) _____   (X) _____

(L) _____   (Y) _____

(M) _____

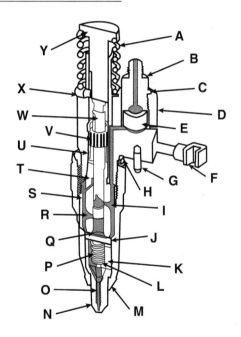

9. The use of a(n) _____ accomplishes metering and   9. _____
   timing during fuel injection.

   (A) upper and lower helix machined in the lower end
   of the injection plunger

   (B) metering valve located in the fuel jumper pipes

   (C) hydraulic head mounted on the fuel manifold

   (D) mechanical governor

10. The continuous flow of fuel through the injector prevents _____ _____ from forming in the fuel system.

10. _____

11. Name the two factors that affect the fuel output of the unit injector.

_____

_____

12. Technician A says that one of the advantages of unit injectors is that they are readily interchangeable between engines. Technician B says if more than one type of injector is installed in an engine, serious engine damage can occur. Who is right?

12. _____

    (A) A only.

    (B) B only.

    (C) Both A & B.

    (D) Neither A nor B.

13. To access the unit injectors, the _____ is removed.

13. _____

    (A) fuel manifold

    (B) intake manifold

    (C) cylinder head cover

    (D) cylinder head

14. Each unit injector mounts into a _____ located in the cylinder head.

14. _____

    (A) threaded bore

    (B) wet liner

    (C) steel sheath

    (D) copper tube

15. The unit injector is held in the correct position by a _____.

15. _____

    (A) dowel pin

    (B) metal clamp

    (C) locator key

    (D) rocker arm

16. The needle valve of the injectors open at pressures between _____.

16. _____

    (A) 1200–2200 psi

    (B) 2300–3200 psi

    (C) 3300–4200 psi

    (D) 4300–5000 psi

Name _____

17. A _____ nozzle design prevents diesel fuel from dribbling into the combustion chamber after injection is complete.

    (A) check valve

    (B) needle valve

    (C) valve cover orifice

    (D) fast-acting

17. _____

18. Technician A says that all models of unit injectors are manufactured to perform within a given fuel flow range. Technician B says that all injectors on a given engine can have different flow rates as long as they fall within the specified range for the engine model. Who is right?

    (A) A only.

    (B) B only.

    (C) Both A & B.

    (D) Neither A nor B.

18. _____

19. Once the injector is installed in the cylinder head, a specific _____ _____ of the injector follower above the body must be set using a timing pin dial gauge.

19. _____

20. Which of the following statements regarding electronic unit injection is *not* true?

    (A) Fuel not used for injection cools and lubricates the injector before being returned to the supply tank.

    (B) Electronic unit injection uses piezoelectric actuators to create the pressures needed for injection.

    (C) Fuel metering is controlled by the ECM.

    (D) A solenoid-operated poppet valve controls fuel flow into the injector.

20. _____

21. _____ _____ unit injectors use high-pressure engine oil to provide the force needed for injection.

21. _____

22. Which of the following injector types delivers fuel to the combustion in two stages?

    (A) Split-shot injector.

    (B) Mechanical unit injector.

    (C) Electronic unit injector.

    (D) None of the above.

22. _____

23. Which of the following methods can be used to isolate
a faulty injector on a modern four-stroke engine unit
injector?

    (A) Short out each injector using a pry bar to hold the
injector follower down while the engine idles.

    (B) Measure the individual exhaust manifold outlet
temperatures using a contact pyrometer.

    (C) Both A & B.

    (D) None of the above.

23. _____

24. A(n) _____ _____ _____ check measures the volume of
fuel returning to the tank in a given time.

24. _____

25. What is the most likely cause of low-fuel-volume return to the fuel tank?

_____

Engine Tune-Up Procedure

26. The overhead camshaft design of the series 60 engine
eliminates the need for _____ and lifters.

26. _____

27. List the tune-up checks and adjustments needed on a Detroit Diesel series 60 four-stroke
engine.

_____

_____

28. Intake and exhaust valve clearance and fuel injector
height are adjusted by means of an adjusting set
screw and locknut located at the valve end of the

_____ _____.

28. _____

29. Technician A makes valve clearance and injector
timing adjustments when the engine is cold.
Technician B sets the valves and the injector height on
the same cylinder at the same time. Who is right?

    (A) A only.

    (B) B only.

    (C) Both A & B.

    (D) Neither A nor B.

29. _____

30. Intake and exhaust valve adjustment is needed only
when the clearance between the end of the self-
centering valve button at the end of the rocker arm and
the _____ _____ _____ are outside of the specifications
listed in the engine manual.

30. _____

Name _____

31. What two tools can be used to check and adjust the valve clearances?

    _____

    _____

32. The fuel injector height is adjusted using a special
    injector height gauge that is inserted into a height
    gauge pilot hole, provided in the _____.

    32. _____

    (A) rocker arm
    (B) valve body
    (C) cylinder head
    (D) fuel injector body

Name _____

Date _____

Instructor _____

Score _____ Text pages 435–462

Chapter 22

Basics of Electricity

After studying this chapter and completing supplemental exercises, you will be able to:

- Explain what electrical current is and what force causes it to flow or move from one point to another.
- Define and explain how current, voltage, and resistance are measured.
- Explain conventional theory versus electron theory of current flow.
- State Ohm's law and describe how it is used to determine voltage, current, and resistance in a dc circuit.
- Define conductors and insulators.
- Describe the three types of circuits used in electrical systems.
- Describe what occurs in closed, open, and shorted circuits.
- Describe the operation of electrical system components.
- Describe the proper safety precautions required for servicing, testing, and charging batteries.
- Perform battery state of charge and capacity tests.
- Properly recharge batteries using either fast or slow charge methods.
- Properly jump-start vehicles equipped with either 12-volt or 12- to 24-volt electrical systems.
- Describe the operation of basic semiconductor devices such as transistors and diodes.

Principles of Electricity

1. What are the three basic units found in all atoms?

_____

_____

_____

2. Which of the following terms is defined as a directed flow of electrons from atom to atom within a conductor?

2. _____

   (A) Magnetism.

   (B) Electric current.

   (C) Electrical charge.

   (D) Conductivity.

3. According to the _____ theory of current flow, movement of electrons is haphazard rather than in one direction only.

3. _____

4. Technician A says that direct current is the type of current commonly used in automotive and diesel truck circuits. Technician B says that direct current may be produced by the engine's alternator. Who is right?

4. _____

   (A) A only.

   (B) B only.

   (C) Both A & B.

   (D) Neither A nor B.

5. _____ current can be stored in a battery.

5. _____

6. The pressure behind the electron flow is referred to as _____.

6. _____

7. The difference in the potential energy between two points is called _____.

7. _____

   (A) electromagnetic force

   (B) positive-negative force

   (C) electromotive force

   (D) differential force

8. An ohm is the _____ that will allow one ampere to flow when the potential equals one volt.

8. _____

9. According to Ohm's law, voltage is obtained by _____ current and resistance.

9. _____

10. What effect do dirt and corrosion have on a typical circuit connection?

_____

11. Any material that offers very low resistance to electron flow is called a(n) _____.

11. _____

Name _____

12. Which of the following materials is *not* considered a good conductor?

    (A) Gold.

    (B) Copper.

    (C) Glass.

    (D) Aluminum.

12. _____

13. A good _____ is any material that provides high resistance to electron flow.

13. _____

14. What insulating material is most commonly used in automotive and truck electrical systems today?

_____

Electrical Circuits

15. What are the three basic types of circuits found in electrical systems?

_____

_____

_____

16. An electrical or wiring diagram composed of standardized electrical symbols is referred to as a(n) _____.

16. _____

17. A(n) _____ is used to measure the amount of voltage needed to overcome resistance in different parts of a circuit.

17. _____

18. Total resistance in a series circuit may be found through _____.

    (A) multiplication

    (B) addition

    (C) division

    (D) addition and division

18. _____

19. Technician A says that the amount of current (amps) flowing through each resistor in a series circuit will not be the same. Technician B says that if one branch of a series circuit breaks, the others will still continue to operate. Who is right?

    (A) A only.

    (B) B only.

    (C) Both A & B.

    (D) Neither A nor B.

19. _____

20. Total resistance in a(n) _____-_____ circuit is found by adding the sum total of the series portion resistance to the sum total of the parallel portion resistance.

20. _____

21. When the negative terminal of the battery is connected to the metal frame of a vehicle, this forms a(n) _____ _____ circuit.

21. _____

22. A(n) _____ circuit occurs when there is a break in the wire or wire connection at a load.

22. _____

23. Melted insulation, blown fuses, and even fire can be the result of a _____.
    (A) short to ground
    (B) Zener diode
    (C) improperly wired cold starting aids
    (D) bimetal switches

23. _____

24. Which of the following is the most frequent cause of high resistance in a circuit?
    (A) Loose connectors.
    (B) Dirty or corroded connectors.
    (C) Damaged connectors.
    (D) Improperly installed connectors.

24. _____

Electrical System Components

25. Electrical wire _____ is determined by the load it must carry and the distance from power source to the load.
    (A) gage
    (B) material
    (C) length
    (D) stranding

25. _____

26. According to American Wire Gage standards, the smaller the number rating, the _____ the gage of the wire.

26. _____

27. Electrical wiring is often assembled into groups called _____.
    (A) shields
    (B) cables
    (C) harnesses
    (D) bundles

27. _____

Name _____

28. The solid state components typically used in today's computerized engine control systems are mounted on

    _____ _____ _____.

28. _____

29. A(n) _____ consists of a low-melting point strip of metal enclosed in a glass or plastic housing.

29. _____

30. Technician A says that automatic circuit breakers are often used in systems where safety is vital, such as vehicle headlights. Technician B says that manual circuit breakers are typically used in stationary applications. Who is right?

    (A) A only.

    (B) B only.

    (C) Both A & B.

    (D) Neither A nor B.

30. _____

31. If a switch has two wires running into it and one circuit running out of it, it is referred to as _____.

    (A) double-pole, single-throw

    (B) double-throw, single-pole

    (C) single-pole, single-throw

    (D) double-throw, double-pole

31. _____

32. Because they are temperature sensitive, _____ switches are commonly used as sensors in a vehicle's cooling system.

    (A) mercury

    (B) relay

    (C) bipolar

    (D) bimetal

32. _____

33. A type of electromagnet used to convert electrical power into mechanical movement is called a(n) _____.

    (A) relay

    (B) solenoid

    (C) fusible link

    (D) armature

33. _____

34. Most modern trucks and vehicles now use a fuse panel or junction block assembly containing blade-type plug-in fuses. Larger blade fuses are also used and are referred to as _____.

    (A) fusible link

    (B) mercury switch

    (C) resistor

    (D) Maxi fuses or Pacific fuses

34. _____

Batteries

35. When connected to an electrical source, a reaction occurs in a battery that converts _____ energy to electrical energy.

35. _____

36. Each element in a battery is immersed in a(n) _____ solution composed of water (H_2O) and sulfuric acid (H_2SO_4).

36. _____

37. A battery element becomes a(n) _____ once it is placed in electrolyte and becomes chemically active.

37. _____

38. Each battery cell typically has an open circuit voltage of approximately _____ volts.

    (A) 1.2

    (B) 1.8

    (C) 2.1

    (D) 2.8

38. _____

39. The battery's state of charge may be determined by measuring the specific gravity of its electrolyte with a(n) _____.

    (A) hydrometer

    (B) voltmeter

    (C) ammeter

    (D) ohmmeter

39. _____

40. When used in battery plate grids, _____ is the cause of most of the hydrogen and oxygen gassing during normal operation.

    (A) copper

    (B) antimony

    (C) calcium

    (D) strontium

40. _____

Name _____

41. A(n) _____-_____ battery is a sealed battery that has no cell caps for adding water.

41. _____

42. A battery's cold cranking performance is a measure of _____.
    (A) number of cells
    (B) service life
    (C) discharge load
    (D) voltage

42. _____

43. The battery's _____ capacity indicates how long it could supply power to the electrical system in the event of a charging system malfunction.

43. _____

44. At 0°F (-18°C), a fully charged battery will have _____ of its potential capacity.
    (A) 75%
    (B) 60%
    (C) 40%
    (D) 25%

44. _____

45. The _____ battery cable should always be removed first.

45. _____

46. Incorrect connection of cables during in-vehicle charging can damage a vehicle's _____.

46. _____

47. Batteries can be grouped into four major types. What are they?

_____

_____

_____

_____

Battery Preventive Maintenance

48. Corrosion can be best removed from a battery terminal using _____.
    (A) engine oil
    (B) vinegar
    (C) baking soda and water
    (D) a mild detergent solution

48. _____

49. If battery cells can be accessed, fill them to 1/2″ above the top of the grid plates with _____.
    (A) electrolyte
    (B) distilled water
    (C) deionized water
    (D) Either A or B.

49. _____

Battery Testing and Service

50. What two tests should be performed whenever a battery is suspected of being weak?
    _____
    _____

51. When taking a hydrometer reading, the lower the float ball sinks in the electrolyte, _____.
    (A) the lower the electrolyte specific gravity
    (B) the lower the battery state of charge
    (C) the greater the battery state of charge
    (D) Both A & B.

51. _____

52. Describe hydrometer readings that would indicate a sufficiently charged battery.
    _____
    _____
    _____

53. With a built-in battery hydrometer, the appearance of a green dot indicates _____.
    (A) 65% or more of charge
    (B) 65% or less of charge
    (C) dead battery
    (D) fully charged battery

53. _____

54. How is an open circuit voltage test performed?
    _____

55. How do you remove a surface charge from a freshly charged battery?
    _____

56. A(n) _____ test determines how well the battery will function under load.

56. _____

Name _____

57. Never perform a capacity test on a sealed battery at   57. _____
    temperatures below _____.
    (A) 50°F
    (B) 60°F
    (C) 72°F
    (D) 80°F

58. Name the three components contained in a battery tester.

    _____

    _____

    _____

59. The current load placed on a battery during a battery   59. _____
    load test should be maintained for _____.
    (A) 5 seconds
    (B) 15 seconds
    (C) 30 seconds
    (D) 60 seconds

60. What information does the key off draw test give to the diesel technician?

    _____

    _____

    _____

Battery Charging

61. Fast chargers charge batteries at a rate of _____   61. _____
    amperes.
    (A) 10–30
    (B) 40–70
    (C) 70–100
    (D) 100–125

62. What can occur if fast charging is done incorrectly?

    _____

63. Most maintenance-free batteries should be fast   63. _____
    charged using a current rate between _____ amperes.

64. Trickle, or slow, chargers often take up to _____ hours to fully charge a battery.
    (A) 10
    (B) 24
    (C) 40
    (D) 60

64. _____

65. Never charge a maintenance-free battery that gives a(n) _____ hydrometer reading.
    (A) green
    (B) red
    (C) black
    (D) clear/light yellow

65. _____

66. Name the three ways multiple batteries can be connected to create desired voltage and/or CCA ratings.

    _____

    _____

    _____

67. When two batteries are connected in parallel, cold cranking amperage _____.
    (A) increases by a factor of two
    (B) decreases by one-half
    (C) remains unchanged
    (D) increases by a factor of four

67. _____

68. When two batteries are connected in parallel, voltage _____.
    (A) increases by a factor of two
    (B) decreases by one-half
    (C) remains unchanged
    (D) increases by a factor of four

68. _____

69. Series-parallel battery hook-ups can _____ both voltage and CCA ratings.

69. _____

70. When jump-starting an engine, the booster battery must be _____.
    (A) the same voltage as the dead battery
    (B) the same or greater voltage as the dead battery
    (C) any standard voltage, even if less than the dead battery
    (D) at room temperature

70. _____

Name _____

71. When jump-starting, Technician A makes certain
    that the vehicles involved do not touch an undesired
    ground. Technician B disconnects all engine and brake
    electronic systems. Who is right?

    (A) A only.

    (B) B only.

    (C) Both A & B.

    (D) Neither A nor B.

71. _____

72. One end of a jumper cable is attached to the negative (ground) terminal of the booster
    battery. What is the other end of this cable connected to?

    _____

73. The maximum amount of time you should crank
    an engine before resting the starter for two minutes
    is _____.

73. _____

74. A remote positive connection point that is easily
    accessed with jumper cables is called a _____.

    (A) jump-start log

    (B) Kettering connection

    (C) rheostat

    (D) jump-start lug

74. _____

Semiconductor Devices

75. When atoms share electrons in covalent bonds,
    they create a structure with a lattice-like appearance
    commonly referred to as a(n) _____.

    (A) web

    (B) crystal

    (C) weave

    (D) lattice

75. _____

76. Crystals are very _____ electrical structures.

    (A) stable

    (B) unstable

    (C) disorganized

    (D) unpredictable

76. _____

77. Semiconductor conductivity can be dramatically
    increased by a process known as _____, which
    involves adding other materials or impurities to the
    silicon or germanium.

77. _____

78. A diode made of silicon generally has a barrier voltage of approximately _____ volts.

    (A) 0.1

    (B) 0.3

    (C) 0.7

    (D) 0.9

78. _____

79. Whenever the negative terminal of a battery is connected to the N-side of a diode, current can flow through the diode. Diodes set up in this manner are said to have a(n) _____ bias.

    (A) neutral

    (B) forward

    (C) reverse

    (D) negative

79. _____

80. What makes a Zener diode unique?

    _____

    _____

81. Name the two types of transistors.

    _____

    _____

82. Name the three regions of a transistor.

    _____

    _____

    _____

83. Transistors have insulating and conductive abilities that allow them to act as _____.

83. _____

84. A very small amount of current applied to the _____ of a transistor allows a very large amount of current to flow through it.

    (A) base

    (B) emitter

    (C) collector

    (D) Either B or C.

84. _____

Name _____

Date _____

Instructor _____

Score _____ Text pages 463–494

Chapter 23

Electronic Engine Controls and Fuel Injection

After studying this chapter and completing supplemental exercises, you will be able to:

- Explain the operating principles of basic electronic components.
- Describe the operating principles of an electronic engine control system, including the role of sensors, computers, and actuators.
- Describe the basic operation of engine control computers, including A/D converters, ROM, RAM, PROM, EPROM, EEPROM, and FEPROM memory, and clock chips.
- Explain how on-board engine computers communicate with other control modules, personal computers, and service tools.
- Define what a software program is, what it does, and give examples of the types of programs used by service technicians and fleet managers.
- Explain the basic operating principles of high-pressure common rail (HPCR) systems.
- Define and give examples of factory and customer programmable diesel control system parameters.
- Give brief overviews of the electronic engine control systems offered by several major manufacturers.
- Describe the basic steps used when troubleshooting engines equipped with electronic controls.

Diesel Engine Control Systems

1. Name three components or characteristics shared by all electronic engine control systems.

_____

_____

_____

2. Technician A says modern diesel engines and
on-highway trucks may use more than one
controller to control all engine and vehicle functions.
Technician B says one disadvantage of multiple
controllers is their inability to communicate and work
together as a system. Who is right?

(A) A only.

(B) B only.

(C) Both A & B.

(D) Neither A nor B.

2. _____

Electronic Control Module

3. The _____ _____ _____ is the brain for the engine
control system.

3. _____

4. The ECM uses _____ _____ as communication signals.

4. _____

5. Most sensors use a reference voltage in the _____
range.

(A) 1–2 volt

(B) 3–4 volt

(C) 5–9 volt

(D) 10–12 volt

5. _____

6. Name the two types of voltage signals.

_____

_____

7. Which type of voltage signal varies continuously over a given range?

_____

8. Digital signals are matched to a(n) _____ number code,
which is the language the ECM uses to communicate.

8. _____

9. The _____ _____ circuit protects the ECM's electronic
components from shorts and the higher voltages of the
external circuits.

9. _____

10. In the ECM, a quartz crystal acts as a(n) _____ to
produce a continuous, timed pulse.

10. _____

11. A(n) _____ is a set of instructions for the ECM.

11. _____

Name _____

12. What type of vehicle computer memory is used to
store permanent information and data?
    (A) Read only memory (ROM).
    (B) Random access memory (RAM).
    (C) Hard drive memory.
    (D) CD memory.

12. _____

13. What do the following acronyms stand for?
    PROM _____
    EPROM _____
    EEPROM _____

14. What type of memory can be erased and its data
reprogrammed?
    (A) PROM.
    (B) EEPROM.
    (C) EPROM.
    (D) Both B & C.

14. _____

15. Customized instructions that are programmed into
engine control computers are called _____.
    (A) downloads
    (B) parameters
    (C) bytes
    (D) inputs

15. _____

16. Any device or system that generates a(n) _____ _____
has the potential to disrupt the operation of electronic
components, devices, and systems in its vicinity.

16. _____

17. Name the most common source of radio frequency interference (RFI).

    _____

18. _____ _____ _____ are used as the standard
communication link between on-board computers and
off-board service and fleet management equipment.

18. _____

19. To allow drivers and technicians to perform data
downloads from ECM memory without a PC or
scan tool, some control systems can be tied into

    _____ _____ _____ _____.

19. _____

Input Sensors

20. _____ are used to monitor a mechanical condition such
as movement or position, temperature, or pressure.

20. _____

21. List five types of input sensors found on diesel engines.

_____

_____

_____

_____

_____

22. The _____ is the most common type of variable resistor   22. _____
    sensor.

23. Name two engine functions affected by coolant temperature sensor input.

_____

_____

24. The oil temperature sensor input helps the computer   24. _____
    set the correct _____ _____ and injection timing.

25. Name two sensors whose input can allow the ECM to shut down the engine to prevent damage.

_____

_____

26. The engine position sensor is an example of   26. _____
    a _____.
    (A) pulse counting sensor
    (B) variable resistance sensor
    (C) three-wire sensor
    (D) two-wire sensor

27. Technician A says the barometric pressure sensor on   27. _____
    a diesel engine is the same as the manifold absolute
    pressure sensor found on most gasoline engines.
    Technician B says this sensor is used to measure
    outside air pressure. Who is right?
    (A) A only.
    (B) B only.
    (C) Both A & B.
    (D) Neither A nor B.

28. The _____ _____ _____ sensor, which measures   28. _____
    turbocharger boost pressure, is used to help calculate
    the amount of air entering the engine so the amount of
    fuel injected can be increased or decreased as needed.

29. Name two engine functions influenced by the vehicle speed sensor input.

_____

_____

Name _____

30. Input from which two sensors will deactivate cruise control?

_____

_____

Output Devices

31. What is the job of the computer control systems output devices?

_____

_____

32. Name three examples of output devices.

_____

_____

_____

Electronically Controlled Fuel Injection Systems

33. Fuel pressure in the rail of a high-pressure common rail   33. _____
    fuel system can range from _____.
    (A) 100–500 psi
    (B) 1000–5000 psi
    (C) 5000–35,000 psi
    (D) 50,000–100,000 psi

34. List the eight basic components that all high-pressure common rail fuel systems have in common.

_____

_____

_____

35. Technician A says that the fuel tank of a high-pressure   35. _____
    common rail system must be specially built to withstand
    extremely high pressure. Technician B says the transfer
    pump pumps low pressure fuel, through a filter, to the
    high-pressure pump. Who is right?
    (A) A only.
    (B) B only.
    (C) Both A & B.
    (D) Neither A nor B.

36. _____ metering of fuel in a high-pressure common rail system involves changing the output of the high-pressure pump to vary the fuel pressure in the rail.

36. _____

37. An electrohydraulic injector uses a solenoid- or _____-actuated control valve.

38. List the three locations from which the fuel return system collects fuel and returns it to the fuel tank.

_____

_____

_____

39. Installing a filter that fits but has the incorrect _____ rating can result in costly fuel system damage.

39. _____

Engine Control System Operation

40. In select situations when a problem is detected, the engine control system will enter a _____ _____ _____ that allows the driver to operate the vehicle in a limited capacity.

40. _____

41. Technician A says on some newer diesel engines, the ECM has the capability of detecting lack of combustion in one or more cylinders. Technician B says if more than one cylinder is misfiring, the ECM will store a code indicating a multiple cylinder misfire. Who is right?

(A) A only.

(B) B only.

(C) Both A & B.

(D) Neither A nor B.

41. _____

42. Technician A says an inactive fault code is one that has occurred in the past, but may not be presently occurring. Technician B says that retrieving blink codes normally requires pressing the engine diagnostics switch on the dash. Who is right?

(A) A only.

(B) B only.

(C) Both A & B.

(D) Neither A nor B.

42. _____

Name _____

43. _____ are designed to show that an electrical or electronic problem has been detected by the ECM.

    (A) Fault codes

    (B) Event codes

    (C) Detection codes

    (D) EPROM codes

43. _____

44. The _____ _____ _____ visually warns the engine operator of conditions that could quickly damage the engine.

44. _____

45. A(n) _____ _____ is simply a list of instructions for a computer.

45. _____

Factory and Customer Programmed Parameters

46. Technician A says diesel engines and the vehicles they are installed in can be programmed only by qualified dealers. Technician B says engines can be programmed to provide desired performance characteristics, track both vehicle and driver performance, and establish automatic maintenance scheduling and history files. Who is right?

    (A) A only.

    (B) B only.

    (C) Both A & B.

    (D) Neither A nor B.

46. _____

47. For _____ deterrence, some systems may require an access code to be entered before the engine can be started.

47. _____

Fuel Injection System Overviews

48. Technician A says the exact number of sensors, actuators, and features varies between different electronic engine control systems. Technician B says that electronic fuel injection systems have changed very little since their introduction. Who is right?

    (A) A only.

    (B) B only.

    (C) Both A & B.

    (D) Neither A nor B.

48. _____

49. Technician A says Detroit Diesel Electronic Controls (DDEC) systems use electronically controlled unit injectors. Technician B says the system uses a hydraulic governor. Who is right?

    (A) A only.

    (B) B only.

    (C) Both A & B.

    (D) Neither A nor B.

49. _____

50. List the four main components of the DDEC system.

    _____

    _____

    _____

    _____

51. The DDEC ECM can determine which cylinder is at TDC and ready for injection to begin by comparing signals from two sensors. Name them.

    _____

    _____

52. Technician A says the ECM in a DDEC I system if fuel-cooled. Technician B says the DDEC 10 system was the first to include a built-in data recorder. Who is right?

    (A) A only.

    (B) B only.

    (C) Both A & B.

    (D) Neither A nor B.

52. _____

53. On Cummins Interact engines, the ECM is cooled by _____.

53. _____

54. The Cummins _____ system combines fully integrated electronic engine controls with high-pressure fuel injection and high-strength components.

54. _____

55. Caterpillar engines designed for _____ applications sometimes come with a software package called Engine Vision.

55. _____

56. Caterpillar Advanced Diesel Engine _____ electronic control system is used on the medium-duty 3126B HEUI engine and heavy-duty electronic unit injected 3604E, C-16, C-15, C-12, and C-10 engines.

56. _____

Name _____

57. In the Caterpillar HEUI diesel truck engine's electronic system, the _____ _____ in the ECM stores the operating information that defines power rating, torque curves, and rpm.

57. _____

58. _____ _____ _____ fuel position is a limit used to control the air-fuel ratio based on boost pressure.

58. _____

59. List four of the lifetime maintenance data totals the Caterpillar HEUI system automatically maintains.

_____

_____

_____

_____

60. Technician A says the HEUI system ECM can automatically calculate and display maintenance intervals based on distance or hours of operation. Technician B says factory passwords must be obtained to adjust the system's configuration. Who is right?

(A) A only.

(B) B only.

(C) Both A & B.

(D) Neither A nor B.

60. _____

61. Mack's V-MAC was a full authority system used on engines equipped with _____.

(A) electronic unit pump

(B) an inline injection pump

(C) a distributor injection pump

(D) individual injection pumps

61. _____

62. What are the names of the V-MAC features that show real-time engine performance data on a dash-mounted display?

_____

Troubleshooting Electronic Controls

63. List in order the seven basic steps to electronic engine control troubleshooting.

_____

_____

_____

_____

_____

_____

_____

64. List at least five tips and techniques for troubleshooting intermittent problems.

_____

_____

_____

_____

_____

65. Technician A says troubleshooting electronic
engine control systems often involves the process of
elimination. Technician B says you should always
refer to stored trouble codes and service manual
information when troubleshooting. Who is right?

65. _____

(A) A only.

(B) B only.

(C) Both A & B.

(D) Neither A nor B.

66. Describe what is involved in a thorough visual inspection of the electronic control system.

_____

_____

67. When checking sensors, what type of ohmmeter should be used?

_____

68. What advantage does a voltmeter offer in troubleshooting electronic circuits?

_____

_____

Name _____

69. Technician A says lack of continuity indicates an open circuit due to a break in the wiring or a bad connection. Technician B says you should always disconnect the wiring harness from the ECM before continuity testing any part of the computer control wiring harness. Who is right?

    (A) A only.

    (B) B only.

    (C) Both A & B.

    (D) Neither A nor B.

69. _____

70. How much impedance should a digital ohmmeter have?

_____

71. _____ can be used as a diagnostic tool on diesel engine control systems to check the waveform patterns from sensors and ECM outputs.

71. _____

72. The latest scopes have _____ _____ _____ _____, which can be used to capture and store waveform patterns.

72. _____

73. The absolutely last step in the troubleshooting process is _____.

73. _____

74. _____ _____ can build up in your body and clothing and can damage sensitive electronic components such as PROM chips.

74. _____

75. When troubleshooting electronic systems, always check for _____ _____ _____ before disconnecting any plug-in connector in the system.

75. _____

76. Moisture traveling through the inside of a wire is referred to as _____.

76. _____

Name _____

Date_____

Instructor_____

Score _____ Text pages 495–512

Chapter 24

Diesel Engine Charging Systems

After studying this chapter and completing supplemental exercises, you will be able to:

- List the basic components of a charging system.
- Describe the principles of magnetism as they relate to charging systems.
- Explain the basic differences between alternators and generators.
- List the major components of an alternator and describe its operation.
- Describe the principles of ac rectification.
- Describe the operation of an electronic voltage regulator.
- List the service precautions that must be taken when working on alternators and charging systems.
- List common causes of overcharging and undercharging.
- Perform checks and adjustments on the charging system.
- Remove and install an alternator on a typical diesel engine.
- Inspect and service the drive belt and tensioner assembly.

Charging System

1. The job of the charging system is to _____.

   (A) recharge the batteries as needed

   (B) provide current to power electrical loads

   (C) Both of the above.

   (D) Neither of the above.

1. _____

2. When voltage falls below a certain level, the alternator begins producing electricity after an electrical switch called the _____ is switched on.

    (A) flux

    (B) pole

    (C) voltage regulator

    (D) starter loop

2. _____

3. Magnetic flux lines have a _____ relationship to the conducting wire.

    (A) parallel

    (B) tangential

    (C) diverging

    (D) right angle

3. _____

4. What effect will increasing current flow have on flux density?

    (A) Flux density will change direction.

    (B) Flux density will oscillate.

    (C) Flux density will increase.

    (D) Flux density will decrease.

4. _____

5. The resistance a circuit or path offers to the line of flux is called _____.

    (A) antropy

    (B) reluctance

    (C) hysteresis

    (D) None of the above.

5. _____

6. When magnetic fields are used to generate electricity, it is called _____.

    (A) relucted voltage

    (B) conducted voltage

    (C) indirect voltage

    (D) induced voltage

6. _____

Alternators

7. The _____ employs a wire or conductor as the moving element, while the magnetic field remains stationary.

    (A) alternator

    (B) dc generator

    (C) Both of the above.

    (D) Neither of the above.

7. _____

Name _____

8. The _____ employs a spinning magnetic field rotating inside stationary conductors.

(A) alternator

(B) dc generator

(C) Both of the above.

(D) Neither of the above.

8. _____

9. The _____ is moving inside an alternator.

(A) rotor

(B) stator

(C) Both of the above.

(D) Neither of the above.

9. _____

10. The _____ is stationary inside an alternator.

(A) rotor

(B) stator

(C) Both of the above.

(D) Neither of the above.

10. _____

11. The windings of a stator are staggered around the iron frame and wired together to form a circuit that resembles a(n) _____.

(A) delta

(B) wye

(C) Either of the above.

(D) Neither of the above.

11. _____

12. Which type of stator winding would most likely be used in an automotive application?

(A) Delta-wound stator.

(B) Wye-wound stator.

(C) Either of the above.

(D) Neither of the above.

12. _____

13. A small air gap should exist between the rotor and the stator. If this gap is not maintained and the rotor touches the stator, the alternator will _____.

(A) produce too much voltage

(B) produce too little voltage

(C) produce direct current instead of alternating current

(D) short to ground and damage the alternator

13. _____

14. As the North and South poles of the spinning rotor pass each loop in the stator, they induce _____.
  (A) voltage
  (B) current
  (C) Both of the above.
  (D) Neither of the above.

14. _____

15. Alternator stators contain three separate windings that are all energized simultaneously. This overlapping operation ensures that _____.
  (A) positive voltage, but not negative voltage, is produced at all times
  (B) negative voltage, but not positive voltage, is produced at all times
  (C) both positive and negative voltage are produced at all times
  (D) neither positive nor negative voltage are produced at all times

15. _____

16. Alternators perform the job of rectification _____.
  (A) mechanically
  (B) electronically
  (C) Both of the above.
  (D) Neither of the above.

16. _____

17. Alternators use _____ rectification to supply current to the system at all times when rectifying voltage from ac to dc.
  (A) quarter-wave
  (B) half-wave
  (C) three-quarter-wave
  (D) full-wave

17. _____

Voltage Regulators

18. Voltage regulators use _____ to switch the field current on and off.
  (A) transistors
  (B) Zener diodes
  (C) Both of the above.
  (D) Neither of the above.

18. _____

Name _____

19. Electronic voltage regulators are located on the ground side of the rotor. This type of field circuit is known as _____.

19. _____

(A) A-type field circuit

(B) B-type field circuit

(C) C-type field circuit

(D) D-type field circuit

Service Precautions

20. Be sure of _____ before connecting any battery or alternator for starting.

20. _____

Charging System Problems

21. If an alternator has low voltage output, and the adjustment screw does not correct the problem, a(n) _____ could be a possible cause.

21. _____

(A) defective voltage regulator

(B) defective diode trio

(C) Both of the above.

(D) Neither of the above.

22. A(n) _____ could cause a battery to overcharge.

22. _____

(A) defective battery

(B) defective or poorly adjusted voltage regulator

(C) bad sensing lead contact to the voltage regulator

(D) All of the above.

23. When testing a voltage regulator using the full-field test, the alternator should be full-fielded for a maximum of _____.

23. _____

(A) 2–3 seconds

(B) 10–15 seconds

(C) 30–45 seconds

(D) 60 seconds

24. When using a digital ohmmeter to test a diode, which would indicate a good diode when the leads are reversed?

24. _____

(A) No reading either direction.

(B) Same reading either direction.

(C) One direction reads higher than the other.

(D) None of the above.

Name _____

Date_____

Instructor_____

Score_____ Text pages 513–530

Chapter 25

Diesel Starting Systems

After studying this chapter and completing supplemental exercises, you will be able to:

- Name the five major components of a diesel engine electrical starting system.
- Describe the two major circuits used in an electrical starting system and how they operate.
- Understand how an electric starting motor operates.
- Perform starter system tests.
- Describe no-load testing of the starter system.
- Explain the basic operating principles of an air-powered starting system.
- Describe the operation of a hydraulic starting system.
- Name and describe the operating principles of the cold weather starting aids used on diesel engines.

Starting System

1. A(n) _____ starters may be used to crank a diesel engine.

   (A) electric

   (B) hydraulic

   (C) pneumatic

   (D) All of the above.

1. _____

Electric Starter System Components

2. Name the five major parts of an electric starting system.

_____

_____

_____

_____

_____

3. The neutral safety switch ensures that a vehicle with an
   automatic transmission can only be started when the
   transmission is in the _____ position.

   (A) park

   (B) neutral

   (C) Either of the above.

   (D) Neither of the above.

3. _____

4. Name two types of starter designs used for cranking diesel engines.

_____

_____

5. In an electric starter, an armature serves as the
   conductor. It is formed into a loop and its ends are
   connected to bars known as _____ segments.

   (A) solenoid

   (B) pole shoe

   (C) field coil

   (D) commutator

5. _____

6. To form the equivalent of a horseshoe magnet, heavy
   wire is wound around a piece of iron to create an
   electromagnet. The windings are called _____.

   (A) solenoids

   (B) pole shoes

   (C) field coils

   (D) commutators

6. _____

7. To form the equivalent of a horseshoe magnet, heavy
   wire is wound around a piece of iron to create an
   electromagnet. The iron bar is known as a(n) _____.

   (A) solenoid

   (B) pole shoe

   (C) field coil

   (D) commutator

7. _____

Name _____

8. Current is supplied to the armature _____.
   (A) through the control circuit
   (B) through the starter switch
   (C) through the starter frame
   (D) through spring-loaded brushes

8. _____

9. Armature rotation is caused by _____.
   (A) pneumatic force
   (B) hydraulic force
   (C) inertial force
   (D) magnetic force

9. _____

10. Field coil windings are made of _____.
    (A) iron
    (B) copper
    (C) aluminum
    (D) silver

10. _____

11. To ensure smooth, uniform rotation and strong torque, armatures have _____.
    (A) many windings
    (B) multiple insulators
    (C) Timken bearing mounts
    (D) ball bearings supporting the shaft

11. _____

12. Armature coils connect to _____.
    (A) each other
    (B) the commutator
    (C) Both of the above.
    (D) Neither of the above.

12. _____

13. The heavy copper segments of the commutator are _____.
    (A) connected to each other
    (B) insulated from each other
    (C) grounded to the armature shaft
    (D) grounded to the housing frame

13. _____

14. Current is conducted from the stationary field coils to the rotating armature coils by _____.
    (A) heavy copper ribbon windings
    (B) the control circuit
    (C) stationary carbon brushes
    (D) the starter circuit

14. _____

15. During operations, what is the polarity of the brushes?   15. _____

    (A) All brushes are "live."

    (B) All brushes are "ground."

    (C) Half of the brushes are "live," the other half are "ground."

    (D) The brushes are not energized.

16. The motor's field coil windings are wired in combinations of series and series-parallel circuits to increase the starter motor torque or speed. Torque can be increased by _____.   16. _____

    (A) adding more field coils

    (B) increasing the windings on the field coils

    (C) Both of the above.

    (D) Neither of the above.

17. When a shunt coil is used in a straight series circuit to limit the motor's top speed and prevent possible damage, the shunt coil is wired _____.   17. _____

    (A) through the brushes and commutator to the armature

    (B) directly to ground independently

    (C) directly to the power source

    (D) None of the above.

18. A shunt coil works by _____.   18. _____

    (A) increasing overall current flow to the armature

    (B) increasing the strength of the magnetic field

    (C) Both of the above.

    (D) Neither of the above.

19. Many heavy-duty starters are equipped with a circuit-breaker type device called a(n) _____ to protect them from damage due to overheating.   19. _____

    (A) fusible link

    (B) thermal protection circuit

    (C) Both of the above.

    (D) Neither of the above.

20. The solenoid coil contains _____.   20. _____

    (A) a hold-in winding

    (B) a pull-in winding

    (C) Both of the above.

    (D) Neither of the above.

Name _____

21. To engage and disengage the pinion gear of the starter and the flywheel ring gear, an electric starter uses _____.
    (A) an overrunning or sprag clutch drive
    (B) an inertia or Bendix drive
    (C) Either of the above.
    (D) Neither of the above.

21. _____

22. A(n) _____ requires the use of a solenoid switch and a shift mechanism mounted in a sealed case on top of the starter housing.
    (A) overrunning or sprag clutch drive
    (B) inertia or Bendix drive
    (C) Both of the above.
    (D) Neither of the above.

22. _____

23. A(n) _____ is no longer used on electric starting systems, but can be found on some air-powered starter motors.
    (A) overrunning or sprag clutch drive
    (B) inertia or Bendix drive
    (C) Both of the above.
    (D) Neither of the above.

23. _____

24. Many heavy-duty trucks and other diesel-powered vehicles use multiple batteries and are equipped with a series-parallel switch, which _____.
    (A) provides 12 volts for cranking and 24 volts for electric system operation
    (B) provides 24 volts for cranking and 12 volts for electric system operation
    (C) provides the operator with a choice of either 12 or 24 volts for all operations
    (D) All of the above.

24. _____

Electric Starting System Tests

25. During a cranking current test on an electric starter motor, a low current draw could be indicative of _____.
    (A) an overcharged battery
    (B) low circuit resistance due to faulty components or connections
    (C) Both of the above.
    (D) Neither of the above.

25. _____

26. During a cranking current test on an electric starter motor, a short in the starter motor or mechanical resistance in the engine or starter due to binding, misalignment, or failed components would cause current draw to be _____.

    (A) low

    (B) high

    (C) Either of the above.

    (D) Neither of the above.

26. _____

27. During an available voltage test, the minimum voltage drop during cranking of a 12-volt starter should be no lower than _____ volts.

    (A) 8

    (B) 9

    (C) 10

    (D) 11

27. _____

28. When determining if a faulty remote starter relay is the cause of a starter not cranking, a technician performs a relay bypass test. When a temporary jumper cable is connected around the starter relay, the starter cranks. This would indicate _____.

    (A) that the relay is not the source of the problem

    (B) that the relay is the source of the problem

    (C) that the thermal protection device is activated

    (D) None of the above.

28. _____

29. A technician needs to check all of the wiring and components used to operate the starter relay and solenoid. The proper test to perform would be the _____.

    (A) cranking current test

    (B) relay bypass test

    (C) control circuit test

    (D) None of the above.

29. _____

30. The proper meter to use when performing a starter circuit resistance test is _____.

    (A) an ohmmeter

    (B) a voltmeter

    (C) an amperage meter

    (D) None of the above.

30. _____

Name _____

31. For starter circuit resistance tests, all of the following are acceptable ways to prevent the engine from starting, *except*:

    (A) holding the exhaust brake button.

    (B) shutting off fuel to the engine.

    (C) activating the inlet air emergency shutdown.

    (D) All of the above.

31. _____

32. When removing the starter from the engine for further testing, the first step should always be to _____.

    (A) disconnect the negative (ground) strap from the starter

    (B) disconnect the positive (hot) cable from the starter

    (C) disconnect the negative (ground) strap from the battery(s)

    (D) disconnect the positive (hot) cable from the battery(s)

32. _____

Air Powered Starting Systems

33. Air starting systems are often used on large displacement diesel engines because _____.

    (A) they can reach higher starting speeds than most electric starters

    (B) they can crank longer than an electric starter and do not generate heat

    (C) Both of the above.

    (D) Neither of the above.

33. _____

34. Most problems with air motors are caused by _____.

    (A) insufficient air supply

    (B) overheating

    (C) low starting speeds

    (D) insufficient lubrication

34. _____

Hydraulic Starting Systems

35. The chief disadvantage of a hydraulic starting motor is that _____.

    (A) it has a short cranking time per accumulator charge

    (B) it quickly depletes the hydraulic system of hydraulic oil

    (C) it requires extensive maintenance

    (D) it cannot be repaired if it is worn or damaged

35. _____

36. Slow or very brief cranking of a hydraulic starter can
be caused by _____.
    (A) high fluid pressure
    (B) the use of cold starting aids
    (C) lack of air in the fluid lines
    (D) a faulty directional valve

36. _____

Cold Starting Aids

37. To ensure long diesel engine life, when the ambient
temperature has dropped below 25°F (-4°C), making
the engine hard to start, the technician should _____.
    (A) use plenty of ether or starting fluid in the air intake
    system
    (B) change the lubricating oil and replace it with a
    higher viscosity oil
    (C) use a diesel fuel with a higher cloud point
    (D) warm the diesel engine before attempting to start it
    again

37. _____

38. The _____ coolant heater is located directly in the
engine block, in place of a freeze plug.
    (A) circulating
    (B) immersion
    (C) Both of the above.
    (D) Neither of the above.

38. _____

39. Glow plugs, threaded into the individual cylinders and
heated by battery current, are wired in _____.
    (A) parallel
    (B) series
    (C) Either of the above.
    (D) Neither of the above.

39. _____

40. If the engine is equipped with _____, starting fluids
must never be used.
    (A) glow plugs
    (B) an electric coil air intake heater
    (C) Either of the above.
    (D) Neither of the above.

40. _____

Name _____

41. Using spray cans of ether is dangerous because too
much ether can cause _____.

    41. _____

  (A) severe detonation

  (B) hydraulic lock

  (C) damage to the pistons, rings, and connecting rods

  (D) All of the above.

Name _____

Date_____

Instructor_____

Score _____ Text pages 531–544

Chapter 26

Engine Reassembly and Installation

After studying this chapter and completing supplemental exercises, you will be able to:

- Outline the procedures for reassembling a completely overhauled diesel engine.
- Explain the proper methods of engine run-in using engine dynamometers, chassis dynamometers, and in-vehicle run-in procedures.
- List the situations when sealer should be applied to fittings, plugs, and fasteners.
- Explain the procedures for prelubrication and preparing the engine for startup and run-in.
- Outline the steps for reinstalling the engine in the vehicle.

Establish Good Work Habits

1. Why is it important to keep the work area, tools, equipment, and all engine components clean during the reassembly process?

   _____

   _____

2. Why is it necessary to follow the manufacturer's service manual?

   (A) Many components must be installed in a specific order.

   (B) Proper torque of fasteners is listed.

   (C) Manuals outline proper use of sealants, adhesives, and lubricants when reassembling.

   (D) All of the above.

   2. _____

Cylinder Block, Sleeves, and Crankshaft Assembly

3. The _____ is the foundation for the entire engine.
   - (A) cylinder head
   - (B) crankshaft
   - (C) cylinder block
   - (D) cylinder sleeve

3. _____

4. Before beginning engine assembly, _____.
   - (A) the block should be placed on a clean section of the shop floor
   - (B) the block should be positioned with the crank bore in a vertical position
   - (C) all pipe plugs, oil gallery cup plugs, and O-rings should be installed dry
   - (D) the block should be mounted on a rebuild stand

4. _____

5. When should the crankshaft gear be installed onto the crankshaft?
   - (A) After heating the crankshaft.
   - (B) Prior to installing the crankshaft into the block.
   - (C) After installing the crankshaft into the block.
   - (D) Before heating the gear.

5. _____

6. When installing the main bearings, they should be lubricated with a film of oil _____.
   - (A) on the wear surface only
   - (B) on the back of the bearings only
   - (C) on both sides of the bearing
   - (D) None of the above.

6. _____

7. When checking the crankshaft for end play, what precision measuring tool should the technician use?
   - (A) Inside caliper.
   - (B) Outside caliper.
   - (C) Micrometer.
   - (D) Dial indicator.

7. _____

Name _____

8. What is the purpose of the gear housing?
   (A) It provides a mounting surface for ancillary components, such as the injection pump.
   (B) It provides protection for the crankshaft drive and driven gears.
   (C) Both of the above.
   (D) Neither of the above.

8. _____

9. To install a reassembled gear housing to the block, the first step should be to _____.
   (A) thoroughly clean all gasket surfaces
   (B) snug mounting bolts, but do not tighten
   (C) install all O-rings
   (D) apply a bead of sealant to all gasket surfaces

9. _____

10. Failure to properly install the piston rings before the piston is installed into the block may result in which of the following?
    (A) Cylinder head gasket may be damaged.
    (B) Rod journal may be damaged by oil starvation.
    (C) Connecting rod may be damaged.
    (D) Engine may burn oil excessively or run hot.

10. _____

11. On a _____ diesel engine, vacuum check the piston pin retainer disks for leakage.
    (A) two-cycle
    (B) four-cycle
    (C) Both of the above.
    (D) Neither of the above.

11. _____

12. When installing piston assemblies into the block, the crankshaft should be turned so that the rod journal accepts the piston being loaded at _____.
    (A) top dead center
    (B) bottom dead center
    (C) 90° after top dead center
    (D) 90° after bottom dead center

12. _____

13. Use a _____ to check connecting rod side-play after the rods have been torqued.
    (A) torque wrench
    (B) micrometer
    (C) dial indicator
    (D) thickness gauge

13. _____

14. Use a _____ to check piston protrusion above the cylinder block deck.

(A) torque wrench

(B) micrometer

(C) dial indicator

(D) thickness gauge

14. _____

15. When installing an oil pump, _____.

(A) any needed O-rings should be coated with clean oil

(B) oil ports should be aligned

(C) mounting bolts should be torqued to specifications

(D) All of the above.

15. _____

16. All of the following are accepted procedures for installing camshafts and camshaft bearings, *except*:

(A) make certain that all oil holes are aligned.

(B) install the front cam bearing first.

(C) use a proper installation tool to install cam bearings.

(D) use an oven, not a torch, to install the cam gear onto the shaft.

16. _____

17. Unless otherwise instructed by the manufacturer's manual, to properly install injection pumps, _____.

(A) the engine should be located on the number 1 cylinder timing mark

(B) the injection pump should be located on the number 1 firing position

(C) Both of the above.

(D) Neither of the above.

17. _____

18. When mounting a cylinder head to the block assembly, the head bolts should be tightened _____.

(A) snugly only initially

(B) in proper sequence and steps

(C) to the proper torque

(D) All of the above.

18. _____

Name _____

19. Push rods and rocker arms have been lightly lubricated and installed in their original positions. The technician should check that _____, before actually torquing the mounting bolts to specification.
    (A) all parts are clean
    (B) the camshaft has been installed
    (C) the camshaft is in time
    (D) the assemblies show no sign of binding

19. _____

Rebuilt Engine Run-In Procedures

20. List three methods of running-in an engine after a rebuild.

_____

_____

_____

21. If the lifting apparatus fails during engine installation and the engine begins to fall, the technician should always _____.
    (A) quickly get help to avoid damaging the engine
    (B) try to prevent the lifting equipment from being damaged
    (C) try to blame someone else
    (D) allow the engine to fall

21. _____

22. During an engine dynamometer run-in, the operator notices a significant drop in engine oil pressure. Technician A says the operator should carefully monitor the condition to see if the pressure stabilizes. Technician B says the operator should shut down the engine immediately. Who is correct?
    (A) A only.
    (B) B only.
    (C) Both A & B.
    (D) Neither A nor B.

22. _____

23. When installing the engine, the very last step should be to _____.
    (A) torque the engine motor mount bolts
    (B) fill the crankcase with the correct lubricating oil
    (C) install and connect the battery
    (D) fill the fuel tanks and filters with fresh fuel

23. _____

24. When using a chassis dynamometer to run-in an
engine in a truck with double bogies, the dynamometer
must be adjusted so that the maximum difference
between axle speeds during testing is _____.

24. _____

    (A) 0 mph

    (B) 2 mph

    (C) 5 mph

    (D) 10 mph

25. Before performing a highway run-in, the technician
should _____.

25. _____

    (A) make sure to retorque the headbolts

    (B) crank the engine over with the engine stop
engaged until oil pressure registers on the gauge

    (C) Both of the above.

    (D) Neither of the above.

Name _____

Date_____

Instructor_____

Score_____ Text pages 545–564

Chapter 27

Preventive Maintenance and Troubleshooting

After studying this chapter and completing supplemental exercises, you will be able to:

- Explain the importance of setting up a workable preventive maintenance program and keeping accurate maintenance records.
- Describe how new diesel engine technology has affected PM procedures.
- Outline the types of tests and checks possible with modern oil analysis and the problems the results may indicate.
- Describe the steps in taking a proper oil sample suitable for analysis.
- Name the number one cause of diesel engine failure and steps to prevent it.
- Outline the procedures for winterizing the engine's coolant, electrical, starting, and fuel systems.
- Name the qualities of a successful diesel engine troubleshooting technician.
- Outline the general procedure for troubleshooting engines with electronic control systems.
- Perform the following troubleshooting tests: locating a misfiring cylinder, cylinder compression check, manometer pressure checks including crankcase pressure, exhaust back pressure, air inlet pressure, air leakage checks, and air box and turbocharger boost pressure checks.
- Perform primary engine checks.
- Use troubleshooting charts and service information to pinpoint the source of engine problems.
- Properly prepare a diesel engine for short- and long-term storage.

1. Which of the following is a good reason to follow a
   well-planned and executed preventive maintenance
   program?
   (A) Reduce maintenance costs by reducing engine contaminants.
   (B) Engines run more efficiently with greater fuel economy.
   (C) Engines run more efficiently with reduced emissions.
   (D) All of the above.

1. _____

Setting Up a Preventive Maintenance (PM) Program

2. Intervals for preventive maintenance should be based
   on _____.
   (A) fuel consumption, distance driven, or service hours
   (B) manufacturer's maintenance schedule only
   (C) whenever it is convenient to service the engine
   (D) None of the above.

2. _____

3. A daily walk-around inspection should be done _____.
   (A) after bringing the engine to operating temperature
   (B) after the engine ends its daily operating cycle
   (C) with another technician
   (D) prior to starting the engine

3. _____

4. Why is it necessary to avoid overtightening fuel line
   clamps?
   (A) It makes them difficult to remove later.
   (B) It will restrict the flow of fuel.
   (C) Clamps will deform, reducing clamping force.
   (D) None of the above.

4. _____

5. Level one maintenance usually includes _____.
   (A) changing oil and oil filters, draining water from the
       fuel tank, and changing fuel filters
   (B) testing coolant additive levels and cleaning the air-
       to-air aftercooler
   (C) Both of the above.
   (D) Neither of the above.

5. _____

6. When new belts have been installed and the initial
   adjustment has been made, the technician should _____.
   (A) save the old belt
   (B) apply a slight amount of engine oil to help the belt break in
   (C) reorder a new belt
   (D) recheck the belt tension after operating the engine
       for 30 minutes

6. _____

Name _____

7. Do not operate a diesel engine with a leak in the air inlet system because _____.

    (A) too much air will cause the fuel mixture to run lean

    (B) too much air may cause detonation or preignition

    (C) dirt and other abrasives may enter the engine

    (D) too much air may cause the engine to smoke

7. _____

8. All of the following are reasons to steam clean grease and oil accumulation from an engine, *except*:

    (A) grease and oil accumulation present a fire hazard.

    (B) accumulation of grease and oil will cause the exhaust to smoke.

    (C) it is easier to detect fluid leaks on a clean engine.

    (D) a clean engine transfers heat more efficiently.

8. _____

9. When checking a turbocharger during scheduled maintenance, the technician notices that only the back side of the wheel is dirty. All of the following are likely causes of this condition, *except*:

    (A) lack of lubricating oil to the turbocharger.

    (B) running the engine at idle for extended periods.

    (C) an air inlet restriction.

    (D) a plugged air cleaner element.

9. _____

10. Once a cooling system and radiator have been cleaned, the radiator should be filled with a mixture of antifreeze/coolant and water. For the best protection against freezing, refill with _____.

    (A) pure water

    (B) pure antifreeze

    (C) 30% antifreeze and 70% water

    (D) 60% antifreeze and 40% water

10. _____

11. When monitoring safety and emission information about a piece of equipment, the Department of Transportation would most likely _____.

    (A) interview the equipment operator

    (B) interview maintenance personnel

    (C) ask to see the maintenance records

    (D) None of the above.

11. _____

12. Although most manufacturers recommend oil change intervals, these intervals may be reduced or extended based on filter arrangement and operating conditions. Which of the following would be a reason for more frequent oil changes?

    (A) Using a bypass filter system.

    (B) Operating the engine in a very clean environment.

    (C) Using an oil additive.

    (D) Using a high sulfur fuel (0.5% or more).

12. _____

13. Extended oil change intervals can lead to _____.

    (A) high soot levels in the oil sump

    (B) premature engine failure

    (C) Either of the above.

    (D) Neither of the above.

13. _____

14. Regular and routine oil analysis can be helpful in _____.

    (A) determining optimal oil and filter change intervals

    (B) detecting impending failures and reducing unscheduled downtime

    (C) confirming the success of a major repair or overhaul

    (D) All of the above.

14. _____

15. Oil samples should be taken from the engine _____.

    (A) immediately after adding or changing the engine oil

    (B) when the engine is cold

    (C) Both of the above.

    (D) Neither of the above.

15. _____

16. Which of the following would cause an increase in oil viscosity?

    (A) Polymer shear.

    (B) Fuel dilution.

    (C) Either of the above.

    (D) Neither of the above.

16. _____

17. Although all of the following factors can contribute to the presence of solids in oil, which one typically accounts for most of the solids found in oil?

    (A) Products of oxidation.

    (B) Particles of worn components.

    (C) Dirt.

    (D) Soot.

17. _____

Name _____

18. Why is glycol (antifreeze) contamination of the engine oil one of the leading causes of premature engine failure?

(A) Glycol increases oil viscosity.

(B) Glycol forms sludge and inhibits performance of oil additives.

(C) Either of the above.

(D) Neither of the above.

18. _____

19. The number one cause of engine failure is _____.

(A) glycol contamination of the engine oil

(B) extended oil change intervals

(C) acidic combustion by-products

(D) dirt entering the engine

19. _____

20. Dirt contamination of an engine most commonly occurs through the _____.

(A) cooling system

(B) air intake system

(C) fuel system

(D) lubricating system

20. _____

21. When an oil analysis laboratory uses a spectrometer, it will detect _____.

(A) wear metals

(B) sulfur

(C) dirt

(D) All of the above.

21. _____

22. The measurement of oil's ability to neutralize acids formed during the combustion is called _____.

(A) TAN

(B) TBN

(C) TCN

(D) TDN

22. _____

23. The test that measures the acidity of an oil is called _____.

(A) TAN

(B) TBN

(C) TCN

(D) TDN

23. _____

Winterizing Engines

24. Winterizing maintenance should be scheduled _____.
    (A) in mid-autumn
    (B) at the onset of extremely cold weather
    (C) the night before the first hard freeze
    (D) in mid-summer

24. _____

25. When using a fuel-water separator in the winter, the unit should be mounted _____.
    (A) outside the truck, to avoid fumes and vapors
    (B) inside the fuel tank
    (C) in a warm, protected area
    (D) between the fuel tanks, below the level of the engine

25. _____

Troubleshooting

26. Which of the following should be used by the technician when troubleshooting a malfunctioning engine?
    (A) A precise, analytical approach using troubleshooting charts and tables.
    (B) A description of the problem and its symptoms by the engine operator.
    (C) The technician's senses, such as sight, sound, smell, and touch.
    (D) All of the above.

26. _____

27. What is one advantage of electronic diagnostics?

    _____

    _____

28. In addition to electronic diagnostics, technicians can use the system's _____ as a tool during engine troubleshooting.

28. _____

Primary Engine Checks

29. Primary engine checks identify common engine performance problems in a(n) _____ amount of time.
    (A) undetermined
    (B) large
    (C) small
    (D) exact

29. _____

Name _____

30. All of the following are primary engine checks, *except*:   30. _____
    (A) check oil and coolant levels.
    (B) check color of exhaust smoke.
    (C) check operation of the engine brake.
    (D) check the rocker arm cover.

General Test Procedures

31. Any preventive maintenance procedures performed   31. _____
    on an engine will be practically useless if the engine is
    missing _____.
    (A) proper compression
    (B) proper air delivery
    (C) proper fuel injection
    (D) All of the above.

32. To locate a misfiring cylinder on a diesel engine,   32. _____
    disable the injectors one at a time. The misfiring
    cylinder will be indicated by _____.
    (A) an increase in rpm
    (B) a decrease in rpm
    (C) no change in rpm
    (D) None of the above.

33. Which of the following could cause low engine   33. _____
    compression?
    (A) Worn piston rings or damaged pistons.
    (B) Scored cylinders or leaking valves.
    (C) Either of the above.
    (D) Neither of the above.

34. Before proceeding with a cylinder compression test,   34. _____
    which of the following should be eliminated as a
    source of misfiring?
    (A) Bent connecting rod.
    (B) Fuel delivery and air inlet or exhaust restrictions.
    (C) Both of the above.
    (D) Neither of the above.

35. Cylinder compression tests should be performed with   35. _____
    the engine _____.
    (A) cold and not running
    (B) cold and running
    (C) hot and not running
    (D) hot and running

36. If a manometer was being used to record an extremely high pressure, a(n) _____ would be most suitable.
    (A) mercury manometer
    (B) water manometer
    (C) mixture of water and mercury in a slack tube manometer
    (D) None of the above.

36. _____

37. When checking exhaust back pressure, a(n) _____ would be most suitable for the test.
    (A) mercury manometer
    (B) water manometer
    (C) mixture of water and mercury in a slack tube manometer
    (D) All of the above.

37. _____

38. When checking air inlet restrictions, a(n) _____ would be most suitable for the test.
    (A) mercury manometer
    (B) water manometer
    (C) mixture of water and mercury in a slack tube manometer
    (D) All of the above.

38. _____

39. When performing an air inlet restriction test, high pressure would indicate _____.
    (A) correct and efficient operation
    (B) insufficient airflow
    (C) excessive airflow
    (D) All of the above.

39. _____

Storage of Diesel Engines

40. When placing a diesel engine in storage for an extended period of time, special preparations must be taken to prevent _____.
    (A) rust formation
    (B) improper operation
    (C) theft
    (D) formation of carbon

40. _____

Name _____

Date _____

Instructor _____

Score _____ Text pages 565–576

Chapter 28

Career Opportunities and ASE Certification

After studying this chapter and completing supplemental exercises, you will be able to:

- List areas in which you can obtain a position servicing diesel engines.
- Name the various specializations in the diesel field.
- Discuss ASE certification.
- List the types of questions and test categories in the ASE test battery.

The Diesel Field

1. Diesel service employees provide a valuable service to _____.
   (A) their employer
   (B) their community
   (C) society as a whole
   (D) All of the above.

1. _____

2. Diesel growth over the past several years has _____.
   (A) diminished
   (B) stayed about the same
   (C) grown very little
   (D) grown tremendously

2. _____

3. The area of diesel service that employs the most technicians is _____.

   (A) companies that manufacture new engines

   (B) companies that recondition used engines

   (C) companies that sell diesel engines

   (D) companies that provide diesel engine service and repair

3. _____

4. Diesel technicians who do engine inspections, preventive maintenance, repair, and adjustment of components are referred to as _____.

   (A) apprentices

   (B) general technicians

   (C) specialists

   (D) engineers

4. _____

ASE Certification

5. For many years, the ASE tests were administered as written exams that required 6 to 8 weeks for grading. Now, all tests are taken on a(n) _____ and graded _____.

5. _____

6. ASE has partnered with _____, a computer test service that provides computer-based testing for a variety of industries and government agencies.

6. _____

7. Technician A says ASE was established to provide a certification process for automobile technicians and to promote high standards of automotive service and repair. Technician B says ASE does this by offering a series of tests on various subjects in the automotive repair, medium/heavy truck repair, school bus repair, collision repair/refinishing, and parts specialist areas. Who is correct?

   (A) A only.

   (B) B only.

   (C) Both A & B.

   (D) Neither A nor B.

7. _____

8. Eight tests comprise the Medium/Heavy Truck Technician certification series. A technician who passes one or more of these tests and has at least two years of relevant work experience can become certified as a(n) _____.

8. _____

Name _____

9. By passing either the Diesel Engine or Gasoline Engine tests and the other six tests in the Medium/Heavy Truck Technician certification series, a technician can be certified as a(n) _____.

9. _____

10. After completing an ASE test, how long does it take for technicians to learn their test scores?
    (A) Six to eight weeks.
    (B) The employer gets to see the test results first.
    (C) One week.
    (D) Immediately upon completion of the test.

10. _____

11. The questions on the Diesel Engine test are based on _____.
    (A) theoretical knowledge
    (B) manufacturer-specific information
    (C) job-related skills
    (D) operational theory

11. _____

12. ASE tests are offered during four test periods each year. These test periods are called windows. Each window is approximately _____ months long.
    (A) two
    (B) three
    (C) four
    (D) six

12. _____

13. Anyone may apply for and take an ASE test. However, to become certified, the applicant must have two years experience working as an automobile or truck technician. Technician A says that in some cases, training programs, course work, or time spent performing similar work can be substituted for all or part of the work experience. Technician B says an apprenticeship program does not count as work experience. Who is correct?
    (A) A only.
    (B) B only.
    (C) Both A & B.
    (D) Neither A nor B.

13. _____

14. An admission ticket is required for entry to the test center. Where do you get one?

    (A) You can buy one at the test center on the day of the test.

    (B) After registering for a test and paying for it on the ASE website.

    (C) By mail only.

    (D) Your employer will give you an admission ticket.

14. _____

15. What is the first step in registering for an ASE test?

    (A) Go to ASE website and create a personal "myASE" account page.

    (B) Select the nearest Prometric test center.

    (C) Pay for the test.

    (D) Study.

15. _____

16. Technician A says the questions on all ASE tests are written by technicians, instructors, and other service industry experts familiar with all aspects of medium/heavy truck repair. Technician B says each ASE test is comprised of multiple-choice, job-related questions with only one correct answer. Who is correct?

    (A) A only.

    (B) B only.

    (C) Both A & B.

    (D) Neither A nor B.

16. _____

17. When you arrive at the test center, what should you do?

    (A) Present your admission ticket.

    (B) Present a driver's license or other signed photographic identification.

    (C) Empty your pockets of your keys, pens, wallet, cell phone, and all other contents and store them in a keyed locker that is provided.

    (D) All of the above.

17. _____

Name _____

18. Which of the following is not an area covered by
ASE testing?

   (A) Heating, Ventilation, and Air Conditioning Systems.

   (B) Electrical/Electronic Systems.

   (C) Preventive Maintenance Inspection (PMI).

   (D) Diesel Engine Theory 101.

18. _____

19. The ASE tests are designed to measure your knowledge
of three things. Which of the following in not one of
those three things?

   (A) Basic information on how automotive systems and
components work.

   (B) Diagnosis and testing of systems and components.

   (C) Cummins and Detroit Diesel engines.

   (D) Repairing systems and components.

19. _____

Name _____

Date_____

Instructor_____

Score_____ Text pages 577–586

Chapter 29

Workplace Employability Skills

After studying this chapter and completing supplemental exercises, you will be able to:

- Summarize the process of applying for employment, including writing a résumé, preparing an application, and interviewing for a position.
- Identify the skills, attitudes, and behaviors important for maintaining a job and attaining career success.
- Demonstrate appropriate communication skills to use in the workplace.
- Summarize the procedure for leaving a job.

Applying for a Position

1. Which of the following is not a proven way to prepare for a job interview?

   (A) Research the employer and the job.

   (B) Take a laid-back approach. Excessive preparation makes the candidate appear stiff and robotic.

   (C) Practice the interview.

   (D) List the materials you plan to take to the interview and decide what to wear.

1. _____

2. When filling out an online application, it is extremely important to include _____ terms for which the employer may search.

2. _____

3. A letter of application should include all of the following,   3. _____
   except:
   (A) your strengths, skills, and abilities for the job.
   (B) reasons you should be considered for the job.
   (C) contact information.
   (D) the salary you expect.

4. A letter of _____ can be written by one of your   4. _____
   references to give an employer a more in-depth look at
   your skills.

5. Technician A says a résumé is a brief outline of your   5. _____
   education, work experience, and other qualifications.
   Technician B says employers are looking for someone
   who will be able to communicate effectively and a
   well-written résumé can definitely help you get an
   interview. Who is correct?
   (A) A only.
   (B) B only.
   (C) Both A & B.
   (D) Neither A nor B.

Succeeding in the Workplace

6. Integrity, confidentiality, and honesty are crucial aspects   6. _____
   of _____ workplace behavior.
   (A) ethical
   (B) hostile
   (C) white-collar
   (D) unmotivated

7. The ability to guide and motivate others to complete   7. _____
   tasks or achieve goals is known as _____.
   (A) practicality
   (B) determination
   (C) leadership
   (D) resourcefulness

Name _____

8. Higher-level skills that enable you to think beyond the obvious are known as _____.

8. _____

9. Taking _____ means that you start activities on your own without being told what to do.

9. _____

10. A(n) _____ employee is always prompt and on time.

10. _____

11. Technician A says that it is acceptable to wear garments on the job that feature inappropriate pictures or sayings. Technician B says good appearance is especially important for employees who have frequent face-to-face contact with customers. Who is correct?

   (A) A only.

   (B) B only.

   (C) Both A & B.

   (D) Neither A nor B.

11. _____

12. Specialization has brought about a number of specific job responsibilities. Which of the following are examples of diesel specialization?

   (A) Heavy equipment technician.

   (B) Truck technicians.

   (C) Marine technicians.

   (D) All of the above.

12. _____

13. Technician A says diesel service and repair requires the largest number of employees. Technician B says General Technicians do troubleshooting, preventive maintenance, and repair. Who is correct?

   (A) A only.

   (B) B only.

   (C) Both A & B.

   (D) Neither A nor B.

13. _____

14. The ability to handle conflict and to prevent it from becoming a destructive force in the workplace is called _____ _____.

14. _____

Leaving a Job

15. Job departures need to he handled in a way that is considerate of the employer. Technician A says you should not leave your job with noticeable anger and hostility. Technician B says you should let the employer know, in writing, by giving at least at a two-week notice. Who is correct?

    (A) A only.

    (B) B only.

    (C) Both A & B.

    (D) Neither A nor B.

15. _____